A CHI
IN
ARCADIA

The Chipping Campden Boyhood
of H. T. Osborn
1902 - 1907

Edited by Craig Fees

Campden & District Historical & Archæological Society

ISBN 0-9511434-4-1

Printed in England by The Vale Press Ltd

FOREWORD TO SECOND EDITION

Ten years ago, as the then chairman of the Campden and District Historical and Archaeological Society, it was my privilege to welcome this small book. Not only was it a pleasure to read but it was also an important contribution to the history of Chipping Campden, especially to C.R. Ashbee's Guild of Handicraft. It was Craig Fees who first appreciated the importance of Mr Harry Osborn's memories, sought out his letters, collated and edited them.

I am then delighted to welcome this new edition for which the now Doctor Craig Fees has again been responsible. Ten years ago he was a postgraduate student in the Institute of Dialect and Folk Life Studies of the School of English of Leeds University, his master's degree at Occidental College of Los Angeles in California having been 'Medieval Theatre in Indo-European Tradition'. His doctorate from Leeds came in 1988, his subject being 'Christmas Mumming in a North Cotswold Town with Special Reference to Tourism, Urbanisation and Immigration-related Social Change'. That 'North Cotswold Town' was, of course, our Chipping Campden.

I am happy to be able record that Doctor Fees's research into the town's history in no way ceased with the publication of his thesis and that he has continued over the past decade to make a major contribution to our local history, especially in his recording of local recollections. We are lucky that he has made his home in our area.

In the foreword to the first edition I expressed my hope that Craig Fees's excellent endeavour would be emulated by other members. This has undoubtedly occurred. Our Society can now boast the publication of a number of books and papers by members, as well as its twice yearly 'Notes and Queries' .

In that first edition I also paid tribute to Miss Sheila Wood's work in indexing the letters, for arranging the details of publication and for distributing the book. Our special thanks should now go also to Kenneth Boardman and to Allan Warmington for making this new edition possible. The former scanned the text into computer, made all the necessary changes and typeset the new version. Allan Warmington has assiduously unearthed the new illustrations and arranged the details of publication.

Geoffrey Powell,
President,
November 1996

CONTENTS

ILLUSTRATIONS

Acknowledgements

18.Photographs 1,2,3,6, Norah Goodman; 4,8,12,13,14, Guild of Handicraft Trust Collection; Programme of School Concert & 5, Allan Warmington; Cover, 10, 11, Felicity Ashbee; 9, Art Workers Guild; 16, CADHAS; 7,17, Craig Fees

EDITORS NOTE TO THE SECOND EDITION

The publication of the first edition of this book in 1986 marked a watershed in the literature about the Guild of Handicraft and about Chipping Campden. Nothing written about Campden or the Guild since this little book appeared, if it wished to be serious, could afford to ignore it.

Mr Osborn was the last living person who could write of the Guild and of its move to Campden from personal experience, and with the quiet authority of a child's eye unobscured by adult romanticism he punctured the dream picture which has underlain almost all of the writing and broadcasting about Campden in this century.

He could do this because Mr. Osborn belonged simultaneously to two traditions in Campden, which, as far as publication goes, have tended to run separate and apart for most of the century. One of course is the Guild tradition, the origin of which goes back to C.R. Ashbee and his writings about Campden; indeed, much of what has been written about Campden, whether by journalists or historians, springs directly or indirectly from the Guild tradition, and takes at face value the Guild myth that Campden was a backward rural village which had fallen into moral and physical decay until it was transformed by the coming of the Guild. The other is made up of the oral tradition of Campden itself, supported by the stories and experiences of the people born or raised in Campden. In that tradition the Guild is simply one part of a rich and colourful history filled with local men and women who travelled the world, fought in England's wars, went mad, struggled through recessions played tennis, built roads, and generally lived the daily life of a vital small country town, going back beyond human memory. Mr Osborn belonged to both traditions, and his memories have a unique quality and an irreplaceable authority because of it.

Ten years after the first edition nothing has been changed in Mr. Osborn's text. Thanks, however, to the generosity of the Historical Society we have been able to add a number of photographs and illustrations, to bring several of the end notes up to date, and to improve the typeface and layout.

Craig Fees

November 1996

INTRODUCTION

First a few words about myself, necessary to establish a background for our conversation. I am in my 90th year but still in good health, have an excellent memory and keen interest in the scenes of my bygone days.

My years in Campden were not many. We moved there in 1902 and left at the end of 1907, so all I have to relate is what I observed during that period.

-CF 20.7.83

Perhaps this curious little fact may be of interest - I am the last living person who worked at the Guild of Handicraft. My father was a member and my Uncle was General Manager until 1905.

-CF 10.8.83

When Harry Osborn died in his home in Ottawa, Canada, on July 15, 1984 at the beginning of his 91st year, he was indeed the last direct link to the workshop of that extraordinary social experiment, which profoundly changed Campden, called the Guild of Handicraft.

Formed in London in 1887 by architect/designer Charles Robert Ashbee, the Guild and School of Handicraft (as it was then) intended to carry out in practice the theoretical visions of John Ruskin and William Morris. Out of the working class slums of East London, feeding cheap labour into vast factories dominated by machine production, was to arise a new kind of workman in a new kind of workshop. He was to be a craftsman, and the items he produced were to be handmade. Machines would be used for the repetitive and brute tasks, but each cup or cabinet, each lamp bracket or crucifix would reflect the skills and humanity of the individual craftsman. Instead of the impersonal and competitive factory floor[1], there would be a group of inter-related workshops, working together on complete projects. The men would learn from each other, be represented on the Board of Directors, take responsibility for decisions in the workplace, and share an after-hours culture of sports, singsongs and further education. The quality of life of the producer, C.R. Ashbee argued, would reflect in the quality of the items produced. Raising this quality, would raise the quality of English life generally. The goal of the Guild of Handicraft was no less than the re-generation of English Culture, through the revitalisation of the workplace.

It was for this reason that C.R. Ashbee cast about for a way to get his Guildsmen out of the city of London with its smoke and crowding, and its man-made ugliness. In 1901 he discovered Chipping Campden, which he called "the little forgotten town of the Age of Arts and Crafts where industrialism had never touched, where there was an old silk mill and empty cottages ready to hand, left almost as when the Arts and Crafts ended in the 18th century." A vote in the workshops at Christmas 1901 carried the decision to move the Guild of Handicraft to this country town, and in the Spring and Summer of 1902 one hundred and fifty men, wives and children made the move out of London to Campden. Harry Osborn was one of the children. Ashbee called Campden 'Arcadia' - in classical mythology a district in ancient Greece, surrounded by mountains, named 'Arcadia' because it was 'older than the moon'. The Arcadians maintained their independence from the Spartans, and lived simple lives devoted to dance and song among their flocks. Campden was to be the idyllic setting for a new age of industry.

As a limited liability company, however, the Guild of Handicraft gradually collapsed, and in 1907 was finally wound up. Many of the Guildsmen, including the Osborn family, lost their jobs and had to leave Campden (the Boys' School logbook of November 22, 1907 reads: "Owing to the Guild of Handicraft closing its works, several children have left the school. The majority of these were bright and intelligent"). The Guild principles, however, survived the collapse of the trading company, and the dozen or so Guildsmen who decided to remain in Campden (including C.R. Ashbee) formed themselves into the Guild of Handicraft Trust. A farm was bought, to enable individual craftsmen to support themselves when trade was slack. The workshops were held by the Trust, and business that still came in for the Guild was shared out among its members. A number of decisions were still taken jointly, and different shops cooperated on certain projects. In many ways it was business as usual.

The 1914-18 War put an end to much that remained of the Guild's formal organisation, including the School of Arts and Crafts (which Mr. Osborn describes in some detail below), and the Guild Trust itself. The Ashbees left the area in 1919. A core of Guildsmen, however, remained, or returned to Campden after the war. Though beyond the period 1902-1907 to which Mr. Osborn's memories mainly refer, the success of these Guildsmen in the life of Campden, and therefore the vindication of much that C.R. Ashbee set out to achieve for English Culture and the working man, can be felt throughout the memories that follow.

This book is largely the outcome of Mr. Osborn's own initiative.

He was born in London on May 16, 1894, and was 90 years old when he died in 1984. When the family came to Campden in 1902, he was just eight years old, and when he left with his family in 1907 he had turned thirteen. His ties to Campden were not cut by the move : as he tells in his own words, the Cotswold town wove itself in and out of the rest of his life. A letter from Campden friend Wilf Merriman enticed the Osborn family to Canada in 1914. Harry came back to England in 1919 to marry Kathleen Grace Warmington in Campden Church and take her back to Canada, and when his wife died in 1978, Mr. Osborn drew Campden increasingly to him. He began an extensive correspondence with his nephew Allan Warmington, a native of Campden, in which memories of family and old Campden naturally cropped up. When Fiona MacCarthy's book *The Simple Life* (on the history of the Guild in Campden) appeared in 1981, Allan Warmington sent it to his uncle, who immediately wrote to the publishers, Lund Humphries in London, asking them to put him in contact with Fiona MacCarthy "as I am connected with some of the events and would like to share my knowledge with the author". This started a detailed correspondence. Ms. MacCarthy shared these letters with Alan Crawford, whose definitive biography of *C.R. Ashbee* (Yale University Press, 1985) was then in preparation. Alan Crawford asked Mr. Osborn's advice on several chapters of his manuscript, and a fruitful correspondence ensued. It was through Ms. MacCarthy also that a leading student of English folk dance traditions contacted Mr. Osborn, and it was through this scholar, Keith Chandler, that I came to know him. Quite independently, Mr. Osborn had also struck up a correspondence with Col. Geoffrey Powell, author of *The Book of Campden* (Barracuda Books, 1982). Mr. Osborn was, to say the least, a prolific letter-writer, and very generous with his memories as well as his photographs, several of which appear here for the first time. In telling me of his death, Mr. Osborn's daughter Mrs. Norah Goodman, wrote the following:

> Dad was very active, both mentally and physically, right to the end and extremely knowledgeable on almost any subject. He carried on a

correspondence with at least four authors who, like yourself, were doing research or writing books. He seemed able to hold his own with these learned types, in spite of not having had any formal education beyond the elementary grades. We often urged him to enroll at the local universities as there is no charge for senior citizens and we felt he would have added to the interest of the other students. But he never did, I think he was afraid of being 'found lacking'. He was a whiz at mathematics too, what a great pity he was never able to continue his schooling, but as you know grammar schools weren't free in those days.

He managed quite well, living alone after Mother died in 1978. His house was so neat the coroner wondered who the housekeeper was, but he would never let anyone help him with anything. The neighbours offered to clear his lane in the winter with their snowblowers, but he was highly indignant and liked to do it himself. He rose about 4 a.m., though on occasion it could be earlier. Once he was out shovelling at 2.30 and the police patrol car stopped, thinking it was someone breaking in at that hour. After Mother passed away he said it was the first time in his life he hadn't had to account to somebody, family or employer, and was going to do as he pleased for a change. And he did. We saw him once or twice a week as we lived quite close, but for the most part he had his own friends and made his own plans.

This extraordinary man was answering questions to the end. A half-finished letter trying to explain Heavenly Corner to me (see page 34) was started on July 13, two days before his death.

Fiona MacCarthy, Allan Warmington, Alan Crawford, Keith Chandler and Col. Powell have all turned their letters from Mr. Osborn over to me, and I have left out very little. Surprisingly enough, in going over similar ground with the five of us Mr. Osborn rarely repeated himself - perhaps because he himself had so many interests, and we had so many different questions. Once or twice he has given two accounts of the same event which fit nicely together, and I have decided to put them together as one. For the most part, however, my task has been to select rather than edit, trusting Mr. Osborn himself to tell his story. To help give a sense of when and to whom Mr. Osborn wrote each selection, I have put initials and date after each one.

AC means the letter was written to Alan Crawford, KC to Keith Chandler, CF to Craig Fees, FMc to Fiona MacCarthy, GP to Geoffrey Powell, and AW to Allan Warmington.

At the end of Mr. Osborn's reminiscences there is a section of footnotes. These are meant to complement, provide a background, and in one or two cases to correct Mr. Osborn's narrative. When I have added anything to Mr. Osborn's text itself, it is in italics, inside square brackets, like this: *[the rest is Mr. Osborn]*

In a letter to his nephew Allan Warmington dated 31.1.1983. Mr. Osborn wrote: "Life as it used to be when we were young is of little interest today." All those who have given their letters to this memorial disagree, and we hope, in this small way, to share with others the privilege of Mr. Osborn's memory.

Craig Fees
October 1985/ November 1996

I

EARLY MEMORIES: LIFE BEFORE CAMPDEN

I remember in London when I was in early childhood there were posters stuck up on the walls wherever you looked. For protection many buildings displayed a sign forbidding the posting of bills on them. At the time I speak of I was no more than five years old, but I could read and write at that time and in my wanderings about the locality I could see these signs prohibiting the practice. There were many of them all saying the same thing on the wall of buildings. They read:

Bill Stickers
will be
Prosecuted.

I think they were bought ready made because they all looked alike, made of wood and printed. Anyhow, I could read them easily enough except the last word I read as persecuted. I knew what that meant, having heard about it in Sunday School, but I wondered why the whole district was determined to persecute poor old Bill Stickers. What had he been up to?

- CF 15.12.83

There is another thing I remember, which most probably is not to be seen any more in these days of rapid transport. This is the Fireman's Box, so called because it was a wooden hut set in the street at various locations in the more densely populated parts. It housed a small crew of firemen and a wheeled extension ladder (fire escape). This was hand operated and mounted on large wheels so that it could be pushed easily by a couple of men to a nearby fire before the regular crews could get there.

There was one right across the street where we lived before we moved to Campden. The firemen there on duty were not allowed to leave the box, except on business. There was the pub hardly fifty yards away but they needed a courier. I was able to fill the bill nicely, as the law prohibiting children from pubs had not come into existence, so I had a kind of verbal contract as official beer carrier for a small remuneration. I was six or seven at that time. There were lots of wretched people with no homes, sleeping in alleyways, on stairways and park benches. Things were tough for that stratum of society. I remember being robbed of a penny at that time by a young woman. If you have read Dickens you will have a good picture, and he was not exaggerating.

- CF 14.4.84

My father was an active worker where the church was concerned. Our church had a very good recreation club also and he was secretary for that. We were taken to church every Sunday even before I could read, in fact I can't remember the time when I did not go. I could not have been more than four years old, not only that, but it was Sunday School in the afternoon. Don't think from this that my parents were religious fanatics, but they brought us up to realise that the greatest riches of this world are the companionship and love of God deep down in your heart.

- CF 14.4.84

This *[the period in England before World War One]* was a unique period in history, as it was the end of a way of life that had existed for many centuries. Nothing much had changed, perhaps the style of dress more than anything. Electric lighting and power even in London was to be seen in the form of arc light only in railway yards and the odd theatre front. We used oil lamps and candles right up to the time we went back to London and then it was only gaslight. The London streets were lit by gas light; a man would be seen at dusk hurrying round the streets with a pole with a tiny oil burner on it shoving it up into each lamp to light the gas.[2]

The telephone was a newfangled curiosity and rarely to be found. I remember being taken at about five years old to a Church Hall. Here there was a large bed sheet on the wall and when the lights were all turned down a man cranked a little machine which showed a very speckled moving picture on the sheet for a few minutes, also there was another machine on a table which gave forth sounds as of someone singing at the other end of a drainpipe.

This was the first that any of the people there had seen or heard of motion pictures or the phonograph. It was like seeing a miracle done. I well remember the mystification of all around me that night.

The trams and buses were all horse drawn as well as road traffic. The

Metropolitan Railway [3] (I am sure you have ridden on it) was all drawn by steam locomotives. Can you imagine what it was like in the stations? The smoke would come billowing out of the tunnel ahead of the train. I can still see it; they burnt coal, of course.

The Boer War[4] was about to begin; I well remember it, and the talk of the new colour of soldiers' uniforms: 'khaki'. Up till then soldiers always were redcoats.

What I am trying to give, for what it is worth, is my own recollections of things at that time. No doubt you have read it all and seen pictures, but perhaps you never had it from someone who was there. These last few years of the nineteenth century were the turning point of all that had gone before to turn rapidly into what we have today, like turning over a page in a book and starting a new chapter.

Even dear old Queen Victoria was dying. I well remember the grownups' concern and anxiety at the time and I recall the night, the dark rainy cold night in January 1901 when she died. Perhaps I should not mention the following little intimate detail of that occasion, but you will understand. Mother shooed us, my two brothers and myself to bed that night with instructions to remember the Queen in our prayers. My elder brother (I was the middle one), thought it would carry more weight if we sang 'God Save the Queen' instead, so we were in the middle of that when Mother came into the bedroom saying 'Be quiet a minute, boys, I hear the newsboys shouting'. She went out on to the balcony and there was the sad news, 'Death of the Queen'.

- CF 15.9.83

II

TO CAMPDEN

The Simple Life

My father was not a cabinet maker. He was an ivory worker. This was a trade or art that flourished for a time in the middle of the last century, when ivory headed walking sticks and umbrellas, for instance, were all the rage. His father, my grandfather Henry Osborn (for whom I am named) was one of the most talented of the art, almost a virtuoso I should say from seeing some of his work. Beautiful sculptures in miniature. All done with home made tools and a foot treadle lathe. The ivory trade however died out in the 1890's and my father not being trained for any of the main trades where openings might be found, found himself at a disadvantage in looking for work. There was no unemployment insurance then. No welfare payment. If one was out of work it was just too bad and we were part of it for a while. Fortunately for us, my father's brother W.J. Osborn, being manager of the Guild, was eventually able to find a place for him in the silversmith shop at the Guild. This was when it was in Mile End Road.

I remember all this very well. I was about six at the time. There were three boys in our family, no girls. My eldest brother Bert was two years older than me. He was crippled, but his hands and arms were all right and he had a clever intelligence. I was next in age and my brother [*Fred*] was two years younger than me. I remember Bert telling us two younger ones that we were all going to move down into the country and he described everything to our wondering ears. He had spent months in convalescent homes in the country so he could paint a very enticing picture of it all. A cosy cottage with a beautiful garden full of flowers and roses growing round the door and we should have a donkey to ride on. In short, we were on our way to the Elysian Fields[5] . This would be about the beginning of 1902. Towards the end of April we got packed up ready to move and the van came and took everything away several days before we left London.

Where we stayed for those days is a blank spot with me. It must have been with some relative but I can never recall it. The day came when we went to Paddington and left for Campden. I was so impatient to get there and start picking wild flowers I thought we should never get there. When we did we went to Mr. Pyment's to dinner. That was about midday. Mr. Pyment[6] was foreman of the cabinet makers. They had preceded us by a week or two. Harold and Arthur, the two boys, took us up a lane to green fields galore, thick with buttercups and daisies, so we did get to pick flowers.

Whatever Mother expected, however, was lacking. She probably had the same picture in her mind that Bert had, but it quickly dissolved when she saw the house we were allotted.

The house was (and still is) No. 6 Sheep Street. It is in a six door row, just off the High Street. There was no garden, just a narrow strip of land about nine or ten feet wide connecting the backs of the six houses with a pump in the middle. At the side of No. 6 was a yard bounded by a high stone wall about eight feet high with a door to the street. In one corner of this was an enclosure with a knee high wall. This was the garbage dump. In the centre of the yard was a small building with six doors, one for each house. This contained what is affectionately known in England as the 'Loo', or rather six of them.

There was provision in the yard for a clothes line, one only. Each house had its own day for the use of that. Inside, Mother found things no better. She took one look at the apologetic fireplace she was supposed to cook on and sat down and wept. These houses were new. We were the first tenants. Mother was not given to tears as you might think from what I have said. She was a very courageous woman and had had a life of worry and heartbreak which she had bravely accepted, but the disappointment here was too much. However, it had to be faced. Our furniture had arrived and it had to be unpacked. I might say that though we lived in the East End of London, Bethnal Green to be exact, it wasn't by any means a slum. The flat we had was in a respectable building in a respectable street. There was indoor plumbing for one thing and privacy for another. They were all guildsmen in these houses in Sheep Street and all felt about the same as we did. Some moved back to London as soon as they could. If this was the Simple Life as Mr. Ashbee had planned, something was missing. The Simple Life was what we had left behind in London when you came to have a look at it beside this. From the housewives' point of view, Mr. Ashbee in his role of a latter day Moses had led us into the wilderness instead of the Promised Land flowing with milk and honey.

It wasn't too bad for the men, more of an adventure than anything, or for us kids either, but for the wives it must have been terrible. In London wherever you lived it was never more than a stone's throw to hundreds of shops and merchants of all kinds. Whatever your means there was always to be found what you could afford, whether in food or clothing, anything at all.

Not so in the Promised Land. There were one and a half butchers' shops[7] , two grocers with limited stocks, a couple of small drapers with very little to choose from. (Take it or leave it). This, I think it safe to say, is what Mr. Ashbee left out of his dreams. If the life was simple for the men it was very complicated and discouraging for the women[8] . I know in the case of my own mother she was never happy in Campden, and never or very very seldom went out. We did most of the shopping for her and she made no friends among the natives. One or two acquaintances, perhaps, but no friends.

The inhabitants for the most part had never been much farther afield than Evesham. They were still speaking the language of the King James Bible. It was 'thee and thy and thou'. We could hardly understand what they were saying and they looked at us open mouthed in equal ignorance at our speech.

- FMc 1.5.81

The speech would have been more familiar to Chaucer or Shakespeare than to us. In place of saying to us 'What is your name?' it was 'Who bist thee'; 'You look cold', became 'Thee looks star'd (starved) to juth (death)'; a woman was a 'ooman', wood was 'ood'. The letter 'w' it seemed was not in the alphabet.

Among kids our own age the lines of battle were soon drawn. When I started at Campden School it was like Nero's circus. The lions were waiting.

There was only a handful of kids with the Guild and some of them were girls, so that before the Campden boys we were very much in the minority, however that did not stop us from mimicking them and vice versa and in a few days some noses were bloodied, my own being one, and here and there could be seen a black eye. The natives liked to come at us two or three to one and I found a ready weapon in those cases which took them by surprise. It was merely shinkicking[9], but it was effective and they eventually let us alone and contented themselves with name calling. 'London pickpockets' was a familiar cry. However, after some months things settled down and we were all friends. Among the adults things were different. They had more sense than to go about insulting each other and so found the natives friendly and helpful.

- CF 15.9.83

Campden itself, I have often thought, was like the Sleeping Beauty waiting to be awakened by Prince Charming in the person of Mr. Ashbee.

Present day Campden is only the ghost of its former self. In those days it had hardly changed in its past three hundred years. There were no water mains, only wells. Street lighting was very precarious, seldom working on account of not enough gas, so that it was usually pitch dark after night fall. None of the present day conveniences had ever been heard of, such as the telephone, radio, TV, motor cars. There had been no outside influences such as wars or tourists to adulterate anything or anybody. It was still in its pristine condition. The news and also advertising to a certain extent was dispensed by a town crier who came round with a bell and 'Oyez Oyez Oyez' concluding always with 'God save the King'. There were three water mills in full operation on the little brook there, which has now been promoted to the rank of river. The River Cam. In those days there was no pretence about it. It was Coombe Brook. Its source is at Coombe near Campden House, the Gainsborough's former home[10]. These three water mills are now no more. They have been converted into rich men's homes and the mill ponds destroyed. This is one result of the influx of rich outsiders on a beautiful old English village, a priceless relic of the past. In the case of the mills I often think of the lines of a song:

'Her beauty was sold for an old man's gold'.

- FMc 1.5.81

We stayed in Sheep Street for about a year until a better house became available. This happened in the Spring of 1903. The new house, after the horrors of Sheep Street was a step towards Bert's picture of a lovely cottage, etc.

Actually it was one, or rather two, of the oldest houses in Campden. Two made into one. They had evidently been derelict for years. Mr. Martin-Holland (he was the financial backbone of the Guild)[11], purchased

THATCHED COTTAGE IN WATERY LANE,
CAMPDEN, GLOS. WHERE MR. OSBORN LIVED.

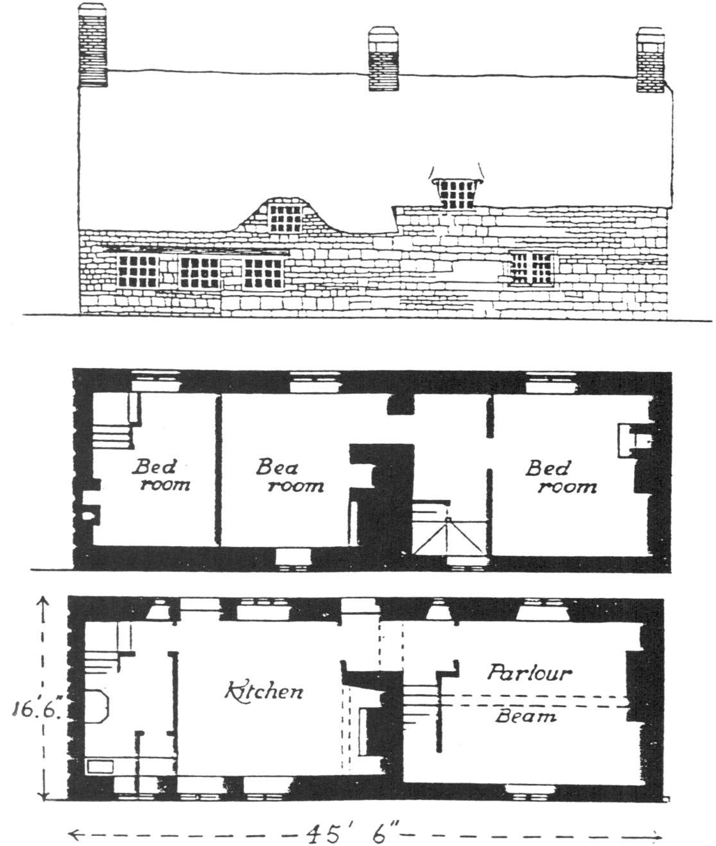

the property and had the two made into one. They must have dated from Tudor times. The walls were very thick so that there was room for window seats in the thickness. They had originally each been one room down and one up, just the typical labourer's houses of those days. Stone floors, thatched roof. When we moved in they had been renewed inside with new floors upstairs and partitions, new staircase in one part, the old one in another. Three bedrooms. Downstairs the large kitchen was partitioned to make a scullery. There was a large chimney corner under massive oak beams containing in answer to Mother's prayers a brand new 'Kitchener' stove[12] . At the back of this alcove was the bricked up door of what might have been a baking oven. The whole upstairs floors were supported by the original massive oak beams. Not only that but there was a suspicion that the place was haunted in a mild sort of way. I say this jokingly. The fact is, though, that the teacups, in lieu of kitchen cabinets, were hung on hooks along the edge of a shelf. Once in a while one of them, for no apparent reason, would start to swing as though started by some ghostly hand. All doors and windows would be closed, no draughts, no vibration, yet just one cup would start to swing and then stop. The house had another peculiar feature. It had no front door on the street, but two back doors. The only house in Campden like that I think.

There was a lovely garden, that is after we worked on it. At first it was just a desolation of weeds, brambles and pieces of old iron, and many stones. Several large apple trees though. Two pigsties and the brook at the bottom of the garden. This was more like it: across the brook was an open view of fields and hedgerows. This was more like the Promised Land and we went at it with a will. We gathered up the stones and father used them to make the long flower bed the full length of the house. The pigsties were perfectly clean. We did not have a donkey, but within a short time one pigsty was fitted up as a chicken run with chickens and several ducks. The other pigsty became the home of a goat. A pigeon house was built and we had pigeons, also rabbits, and cats. When the garden was cleared we had a good variety of garden produce.

In digging one would often turn up big rusty keys and candle snuffers and also the steel for striking on flint to make a spark for tinder. I am sure you have seen them. Also one Roman coin was turned up. I still have it in my coin collection. The British Museum said it was Marcus Aurelius, 2nd Century AD.

I must mention here an august visitor to our house. One day in mid morning as mother was at her morning housework, there was a knock at the door. Mother opened it to be confronted with, as she described it later, a well dressed, well groomed, well built and well poised lady. She was a stranger to mother. 'Good morning Mrs. Osborn', she said, 'I am the Countess of Gainsborough, may I come in for a moment.' She looked younger than her years, a very nice looking person. Mother, of course invited her in, as they say, and talked. I do not know what her errand was. I was not told. Mother, in telling us this said, 'I felt like Cinderella having a visit from the Fairy Godmother.' Her carriage was waiting in the road outside, much I suspect to the curiosity of the neighbours, as the Countess was not in the habit of visiting the homes of the rank and file (we were not their tenants) but was often seen driving past. Her visit may have been connected with something I mention in a moment or it may have been a personal inquiry about Bert. Whatever it was, mother found herself sitting talking to a real live Countess, who really looked the part. I think she was the second wife of the Earl, much younger looking than he was. He was a small built man with grey hair. The family consisted of at least four, all of adult age. The eldest, Viscount Campden, came of age about 1905. There was another son and two daughters. You would not think to see her ladyship that she was the mother of so grown up a family[13].

It was about this time, or perhaps later, that the Viscount expressed a desire, or was pressed into it, to learn some craft or other. Where was there a better place than right in the Guild shops. It was therefore arranged that he should learn a bit about lathe work under the tutelage of my father, turning, of course, being part of the ivory worker's craft. Mother was asked to make aprons for the Viscount, so when this equipment was ready, the Guild found itself with a titled apprentice. This did not last for very long, as the Gainsboroughs spent only part of their time in Campden.

If there was any animosity between them and Ashbees it must have evaporated by that time[14]. Both the Earl and Countess visited the Guild shops together on at least one occasion. I remember my father telling me in later years how they were both conversing with him, and the Countess turned to the Earl with the request that he go away as she wished to talk to Mr. Osborn about his wife. (In present day vernacular, 'Buzz off!').

These contacts must have given us some kind of standing with the Earl as in certain seasons a servant from Campden House would appear at our door with a brace of handsome pheasants, 'With his Lordship's compliments!'

Another notable visitor we had besides the Countess. This was F. L. Griggs[15]. He used to make short visits to Campden before he came to live there and I used to see him around. One day I came home from school and found him sitting in the middle of our garden on one of our chairs. He was sketching the house for a series of illustrations for a book to be published. He was not the author. Mr. Griggs as you know eventually made his home there and bankrupted himself over the purchase of the land known as Dover's Hill, which is now under the National Trust, I believe. He owed many debts when he died, which let some of the people down, but his sacrifice saved Dover's Hill for all time.

- FMc 17.6.81/5.9.81

School

The Building and the Teachers[16]

When we arrived in Campden and started school, we found it, to say the least, somewhat primitive after London. The desks were apparently as old as the building; long forms and desks, black with age and ink, tiered up to three levels. The building contained one room originally, divided into two by a wood and glass partition. Grades I and II were in one part and all the rest in the larger room.

Later on the long desks were taken out, they were almost museum pieces containing the silent history of the inhabitants back perhaps to George III, it seemed. We then had new tip up desks seating two, and about this time Mr. Dewey appeared on the scene. Mrs. Dewey taught the girls' school. Mrs. Dunn taught I and II boys. Miss Lavender likewise the girls.

There was no water on the premises for washing or drinking and never had been until Mr. Dewey had a pail and mug provided, and detailed two boys to go to the Almshouse tap and get a pail of water[17]. This stood in the lobby. As for the sanitary arrangements, perhaps the less said the better. But despite these primitive conditions, Mr. Dewey handled us all pretty well, what he couldn't knock into our heads by fair means he attempted with the cane. Yet for my part at least, though I got my share of his wrath, he had a kindly side. On Friday afternoons towards the last period of study, he would get a book of interesting stories, like Kipling etc., and sit down and read aloud to us like a father, and we never left the school of an afternoon without evening prayers. These are the things that stay with one, long after the pains of punishment are forgotten.

- CF 25.10.83

Our school was much of a makeshift. It consisted of a small building of two rooms. One room contained the first and second grades and was taught by Mrs. Dunn. All the other grades were in the other room and taught by one teacher, Mr. Dewey. It wasn't much of an advance over what Dickens could describe. In winter the stone interior walls would 'sweat', and the water run down in little trickles. There was a fireplace to be sure, but it was away from the desks and had no effect whatever. The desks must have been the original ones, very old and inkstained. They were about ten feet long, with a corresponding long backless form as a seat. Very different from the modern schools we had attended in London. The lower grades were still using slates. After a year or two they got new two seat desks. There was no water until Campden put in water mains. We had to get a pail of water from the Almshouses close at hand. That was all part of the simple life. But I still remember that old school, its teachers and boys, even its canings with affection. Canings were not hard to get. Discipline was discipline in school in those days. Any infractions drew swift and sure retribution, which is as it should be. It had parental support.

- FMc 5.9.81

It was located at the corner of Church Street and Calf's Lane. They call it the Church Rooms now, I think. The master was a tough man and did not spare the rod. He enjoyed it in fact but he had discipline in that school. If any of his pupils passed him in the street out of school hours without raising their hat, he was waiting for them next day in school. Yet I still remember him with respect and a warmth almost of affection. He caned us all regularly but he made us pay attention and learn what he had to teach. We learned recitations, so many lines a week, and he could call anyone to stand and repeat what had already been reached. It was as well to be able to do so. Sometimes it would be a speech from Shakespeare or poem of Tennyson, even a psalm.

We used to have a period once a week devoted to a study of Scripture. That was in the days before God was turned out of school.

I remember one Easter, or rather the day before Good Friday at the Scripture lesson. The master recited to us in his own words the story of the Crucifixion. He spoke as if he had just come from there and had seen it all. The man was a born actor at times, I think. It was so intense and moving that when he finished, us bunch of roughneck boys were many of us in tears.

- CF 10.8.83

The School Concert

The programme you *[Allan Warmington]* enclosed which you so kindly restored and copied, came like a ghost of the past. This is something I did not know existed. Like a ghost from the past it raised up a lot more ghosts. I have very clear memories of those days and those people. The enclosed picture was taken a day or two after the concert. Faded as it is, it may give you a rough idea how we looked.

From left to right standing: Gladys Curtis. (She is the mother of the present mayor of Campden)[18], Alice Keeley (Bad Fairy), Ernie Withers (Santa Claus), Gertie Willis (Good Fairy), Edith Jessett. Front Row: H. Osborn. Anne Beavington. H. Warmington. The doll Anne is holding was borrowed from your Aunt Kathleen[19] .

Incidentally, and I don't blame you for laughing at this, Anne was Harry[20] [*Warmington*]'s girl friend. He always had an easy grace and manner, as you know, and it was effective at his age then. He was no more than ten. He only had to turn on the charm and any girl would follow like a magnet. Meanwhile, I was passionately in love with her too, but I never let on, and in fact you are the only person I ever told this to[21] . Note Harry's attitude beside Anne, and mine. It was the closest I had ever been to her and I was consumed with the flames of love or something, but determined not to show it!

I think I was the first boy in Campden to know Harry. We were living in No. 6 Sheep Street when the Warmingtons moved into No. 3. Harry was still sitting up on top of the load of furniture when it had just stopped at the door and I asked him his name and he told me and said they came from Badsey[22] . From then on we became kind of bosom pals right up to the time we moved away from Campden at the end of 1907. They moved to Campden in 1903.

But to return to the secret story of Anne. The very thought of her yet is something very lovely and tender and sweet, like a pressed flower of bygone days hidden deep down in one's heart, the unadulterated feelings of a boy of 11 for a fairy princess. I guess you may laugh at this, but if you never had the same experience you missed a lot.

- AW 9.6.79

To return to Anne. You asked what became of her. We moved back to London when I was thirteen and I saw her no more. Years later, after I was married to Aunt K, I asked her if she knew what happened to Anne.

Programme

OF A

CONCERT

ON

Thursday, December 21st, 1905,

BY

The Children attending the Boys' & Girls'

National Schools. Campden

PROGRAMME.

PART I.

1. Opening Speech . . . . . . Leonard Lee.
2. Song "Let the hills resound"
   The Boys.
3. Dialogue ... ... "Queen of the Flowers,"
   E. Jessett, V. Parsons, D. Payne, N. Vinn, M. Ellis & K. Warmington.
4. Mirror Drill & Song—The Boys.
5. Dialogue ... ... "Labourers out of work,"
   W. Badger, W. Beavington, H. Byrd, W. Keyte, & W. Payne.
6. Song "The Milkmaids,"
   The Girls.
7. Dialogue "What shall we do when we're men?"
   F. Curtis, A. Keen, W. H. Warmington, G. Ellis
   H. Osborn, J. Tomes, G. Overett & L. Lee.
8. Song ... ... "Eight Little Mothers,"
   The Girls.
9. Dialogue ... ... "A Visit to old Betty,"
   V. Parsons & M. Ellis.
10. Song ... ... Boys will be boys."
    The Boys.
11. Wreath Drill—12 Girls.
12. Song ... ... "The Dunces,"
    The Boys.
13. Tableau ... "The Months of the Year,"
    12 Boys & Girls.
14. Song & Drill ... ... "Topsy Turvy,"
    Boys & Girls.

INTERVAL.

PART II.

A Children's Operetta, by W. C. Ellis,

"SANTA CLAUS."

CHARACTERS:

SANTA CLAUS	Ernest Withers
BIANCA (*A Good Fairy*)	Gertrude Willis
VERDANTI (*A Bad Fairy*)	Alice Keeley

Seven Naughty Boys & Girls—

Louis	H. Osborn
Chas.	J. Tomes
Frank	H. Warmington.
Lionel	G. Ellis
Lucy	G. Curtis
Minnie	E. Jessett.
Elsie	A. Beavington

SONGS:

1.—"Santa Claus."
2.—"What I should like."
3.—"Here we hang our stockings up."
4.—"Night is come."
5.—"I come from the lands."
6.—"Now isn't it strange and queer."
7.—"Morning is breaking."
8.—"Just jumped out of our warm little beds."
9.—"Santa Claus has stolen each stocking"
10.—"A little fairy am I."
11.—"So now we're happy as the birds."

GOD SAVE THE KING.

She told me all she knew was what was told to her and she couldn't vouch for it. It was to the effect that during World War I Anne was a Red Cross nurse and that she nursed a badly shot up Canadian and they fell in love and when he recovered and the war was over they married and he brought her back to Canada. That was the story but I do not know how true.

- AW 24.9.79

The Penny Bank

We used to take our pennies and twopences (those who were rich enough) to school on Monday morning. The school master would make up the list and send one of us down the High Street to Miss Freeman's house with it. So far so good, it was easy to get it in, but to get it out again was something else, it took a budding hero to do that.

First, you gave notice to Mr. Dewey that you wished to withdraw, say, half a crown. He informed Miss Freeman of your rash intent. Later in the week there would be a message from Miss Freeman that you present yourself at her house on Thursday evening at precisely 7 p.m. Miss Freeman's house is known as the Martins and is just behind the far corner of the Market Hall.

There we would approach in fear and trembling, hoping to get the money. The door[23] would be opened by a frightened looking servant girl and you found yourself facing what seemed a vast expanse of dark polished floor across which a narrow strip of fabric was laid to shield it from the footprints of the vulgar. What furniture there was, was close to the walls so that the place seemed practically empty until you perceived a table at the far end behind which sat the redoubtable Miss Freeman.

She was a lady well past middle age, kind of thickset; always dressed in black as I remember, but what distinguished her was her facial appearance. At that time I had seen pictures of grim and ferocious Prussian officers and I always had a feeling that she was one of them in disguise. She looked more like Bismarck, even to a quite evident dark moustache. Beside Miss Freeman sat her second-in-command in the person of Mrs. Morris. She was one of the more monied class and lived in and owned, I guess, the large house in the square, now the Cotswold House Hotel[24]. Why the two of them I never knew, whether they had to watch each other with my half crown or afraid of being held up.

Anyhow, having traversed the straight and narrow line you arrived at the table and felt like a prisoner in the dock awaiting sentence.

Miss Freeman would question you closely as to your identity, also as to why you wanted the money. What were you going to do with it, and why you put it in the bank if you intended to take it out again, an unforgivable crime. I think she persuaded herself in a way that you were asking her to give you money out of her own pocket. When the interrogation was finally over, and she reluctantly handed over the half crown, you hastened out fearful of being pursued and having it taken back.

- CF 19.1.84

Work

Your mention of Gabb's brings back another memory, although I never knew any of them, but after my time they had the bakery by the old elm tree[25]. In my time it belonged to Mr. Heritage. I worked for him for two years as a boy every Saturday, all day, from 9 a.m. until quite often 9 p.m., for the large sum of 6d.

I served No. 3 Sheep Street all the time. Little did I dream that the girl I was selling bread to, I should one day be buying it for.

Well, so much for nostalgia.

- AW 3.1.82

I was eleven years old when I started. First thing to do on Saturday morning at 9 a.m. was to sweep up the yard which took till about 10 a.m. By that time the cakes were out of the oven and cooling. I was furnished with a wide flat basket of rectangular shape and loaded with cakes of various kinds. This I proceeded to cart about, looking a bit lopsided as I went from door to door about the town. That lasted till dinner time. I went home for that. After dinner it was the bread round for a while, while the van was being loaded for the round of villages outside Campden. There was a driver for this but I always went with him. We went to Broad Campden, Draycott and Blockley, through fair and foul weather, Winter and Summer, it wasn't always fun but looking back I would not have missed a minute of it. By the time we got back, stabled the horse and unloaded, etc., it was 8 or 9 o'clock.

My wages? 6d (not 6p). It was not the money, but I think I must be a bit peculiar as I always seem to enjoy work rather than play.

- CF 13.9.83

Play and Celebration

Circuses, fairs, travelling shows

Circuses were not a frequent event. They were only small one ring jobs. We used to receive tickets at school, furnished by the circus of course, and with these and three halfpence we got in for the afternoon show, providing the schoolmaster was in sympathy with us and in the circus mood himself.

Fairs were of two kinds. The monthly cattle show, when the town was full of drovers, sheep, pigs, cows and horses. The boys anxious to earn a penny or two vying for the job of driving various small herds of cattle down to the station, next day having to account for absence from school to a tough and sceptical schoolmaster. It was usually 'Mother was ill and I had to mind the baby'.

The other kind of fair was not so regular. It consisted usually of a few stalls with novelties, cheap crockery, etc. The main thing of interest as I remember was the sale of tubes like toothpaste tubes, a bit bigger of course, filled with water. You could chase your girl all over the place with these. They sold like hot cakes.

The travelling shows were of several kinds, from hand-bell ringers to real stage shows with scenery, drama, comedy and pretty good acting, we thought.

Most of these travelling shows were just one night affairs. There was one, however, that took the place by storm. This was Holloway's Theatre[26] , one of the last of those remarkable outfits now gone and forgotten.

It was mobile to the extent that it could all be packed up on vehicles. The stage itself was the extended floor of one of them. A large rectangular tent housed it all when it was in business. The seats were boards and arranged in two sections, the front rows cost a little more than the back section, which was tiered up like the gallery in the regular theatres.

There was a different play each night, six nights a week, and Saturday Matinee. Real plays, some of them the old tear jerkers like East Lynne, Lady Audley's Secret, Ten Nights in a Bar Room, and the play was always followed, as the poster said, by varieties and a screaming farce. Enough to make two cats laugh!

It was a regular stock company and yet nearly all in the family. Mr. and Mrs. Holloway, their children, Mr. H's father-in-law and several other married couples, but they were all good. The Holloways lived in caravans at the theatre while the rest found lodgings in the town. They were all nice people as far as I know, and well liked in Campden.

The children came to our school, for they stayed in Campden for at least three months. This was in 1905[27] . They even made a play out of the Campden Wonder[28]. This was a huge success, as you can imagine. On Sunday afternoons the place was thrown open to any clergyman who wished to hold a service there. Nobody but the Baptist minister accepted the offer. His church, like all the rest, was more noticed for its emptiness than anything else, but when he went and held service in Holloway's the place was packed.[29] I suppose the fact that you got in for nothing was the main attraction. Mr. Holloway was not averse to devising means to add extra attractions, such as giving door prizes for certain competitions - for instance, the best four line verse about the show. I remember the winning one on one occasion. It went thus,

> Holloway's Theatre has thrills galore
> The best play to my thinking was Jane Shore
> The Campden Wonder was quite a success
> But they played Dick Turpin without Black Bess.

The theatre was set up behind the yard of the Noel Arms in a little plot hardly big enough to call a field. In later times it became a bowling green.

- CF 20.7.83

The circus was in what used to be called Badger's field, which was on the left of the lane behind the Noel Arms Yard. The circus put on a fair show of trained animals, stand up horseback riding, acrobats and clowns. We thought it marvellous of course.

- CF 10.8.83

We thought the clowns very good at the time, and in fact they were, as good as anything I have seen since. They were, of course, painted and dressed up. They had dialogue and much action. These were the days when all entertainment was live, no canned music or films and the artists and performers were the equal of the highly paid of the present day. Even Holloway's had a couple of comedians that could bring down the house today.

- CF 15.9.83

As far as Holloway's theatre went, it was a real entertainment and there was nothing there that you could not take your child or your girl to see. The stage was built-up on a four wheeled vehicle which expanded into a small stage with wings and proscenium arch, curtain, footlights and all, like a regular theatre on a small scale, but quite effective. It was not in the round. The tent was rectangular. In front of the stage was the 'pit' which consisted of several rows of seats. These were just long planks on the level. Behind this was a barrier enclosing a gallery which rose in several tiers of planks upon a scaffolding which miraculously never collapsed. Judged by the present day theatre seats it could be found wanting, but who minded a few aches and cramps in the face of the drama on stage. Some of these travelling theatres were still around as late as 1913. I attended one in Broadway that year when I visited Campden.

- CF 25.10.83

The handbell ringers came from out of town occasionally for a one night stand. I do not know where they came from, but they just performed in the town hall, not around the town.

- CF 10.8.83

Games and Ghosts

As far as children's games went, they were about the same as anywhere else at the time and had not changed for centuries I suppose. We bowled hoops, spun tops, played marbles, kicked balls, played cricket after a fashion, robbed orchards in season. Home entertainment was confined to reading and not much more. Reading for children was much more wholesome than it is now. There were many weekly magazines devoted to good exciting stories for both boys and girls. The radio and especially t.v. have destroyed all that.

- CF 20.7.83

During our time in Campden my brothers and I and sometimes another boy would roam all over the neighbourhood, feeling like explorers in the South American jungle, or Indians tracking white men after reading Fennimore Cooper. We had no cause to fear anything, there was nothing to be afraid of and we went about our expeditions with light hearts. There were good patches of woods around. Maybe a gamekeeper would chase us out, but nothing to fear there.

One day we went up Conduit Hill, and found a little patch of bush we had never been in. It was only a few acres right alongside the road, a fair amount of under-brush. We advanced cautiously on an imagined foe, but suddenly the three of us simultaneously turned tail and rushed out in panic and continued down the road away from the place. When we asked each other what we were running from we all agreed that we felt the presence of some terrible evil thing confronting us. We saw nothing, or heard nothing, but why did that fear strike us in the same second?

- CF 15.9.83

On the subject of ghosts. Nobody seems to know about them in these modern times. There were several regular ones. Marshal haunted the spot where he was reputed hanged and buried. This was at the top of George Lane where it ends at Catbrook Corner. There was a triangular patch of grass at the junction and always a pile of stones was kept on it to keep Marshal from coming up, but he was to be seen at times[30] .

Then there was a white lady down Aston Hill who could be seen crossing the road by anyone venturing along there at midnight. Also down the Mickleton Road there was the Mickleton Hooter. He hooted but was never seen. I suppose they have all been forced out of business and given up. Maybe the white lady got run over in these days of motor cars. These things, though, gave the whole place an atmosphere which perhaps can never be sensed in today's world.

- CF 10.8.83

Interlude : Yubberton Yawnies[31]

Yubberton yawnies went to plough
But when they got there they didn't know how
So they tied the horses to a stake
And all went off to Willersey Wake.

Two Yubberton men to Campden went
To fetch a barrow they were sent
They carried the barrow from town to town
To keep the wheel from touching the ground.

Yubberton tower was always lower
Than Chipping Campden spire
So they put manure around the tower
To make it grow up higher

- CF 20.7.83/10.8.83

December 21st

The mention of St. Thomas' Day[32] brings back fond memories to me. There was nothing of it in Campden, but in Blockley, or rather just outside of it was the lovely Manor House of Lady Northwick in its beautiful Northwick Park[33]. To me this was the setting of all those stories of the nineteenth century where great mansions were the scene. I have read many a one. This had all the requirements: - a long drive-way lined with great trees leading to lodge gates with lodge keeper and wife. The lodge consisted of two parts, one side was living quarters and across the road was the sleeping quarters. I delivered bread each Saturday to the lodge keeper. Their name was Ellis (no relation to Campden's Ellis family). I still have the picture of it all in my mind, walking with a basket of bread down the drive-way to the lodge gates which would be locked, and banging on the ironwork. The keeper would come out with a lantern, when it was dark in winter, and open it up for me. Meanwhile our rig proceeded down the main road to wait for me to join him, via a pathway through the woods, in the pitch dark. It was all so romantic to me. What has this to do with St. Thomas' Day?

Lady Northwick was an elderly widow and an invalid at that time who went out very seldom. She was well liked around Blockley for her generosity and kindness. On December 21st all the children in the district were welcome to come to Northwick and most of us did. We gathered in the courtyard at a certain hour and Lady Northwick would be in her invalid chair at an upper window. We would each be presented with a shining new penny, an orange and what not by a servant as we passed in and felt ourselves guests in a way for a brief period. It sounds kind of weak when put on paper, but to us it was a happy occasion, the walk to Blockley and back was enjoyable in itself. Northwick Park seemed very extensive. To be sure it was not free for all, which added to its dignity and beauty. There was a herd of deer there too.

- CF 15.12.83

I do not remember any school parties at Christmas. The Sunday School had a party in Summer and one in Winter. The Summer one was held outdoors in what was then Haydon's orchard, that is the ground containing the ruins of the old mansion, unless it rained[34]. In that case it was held in the school as was the Winter one, which was not much of a place for a party and as you may surmise, no place for any foolery that goes with children's parties. Mr. Dewey would sometimes attend there with lantern slides. I think the only time I saw a Christmas tree in Campden was once in the Town Hall at a party got up by the Guild for guildsmen and families, maybe the native kids were invited too. Trees were looked upon as too valuable to be wasted as they are today.

There was, of course, the annual prize giving of the Sunday School which took place at one of these parties. The prize was always the same, a prayer book, so that a few years of attendance and getting the qualifying marks would get you a whole pile of prayer books.

- CF 14.4.84

If there were any mummers doing a Christmas play in my time I must have been kept in the dark about it for I never heard about it and I didn't miss much of what was happening[35].

Morris dancing[36] was still alive when we arrived as I saw it performed shortly afterwards, although it was not a frequent occurrence. I am certain that Mr. Ashbee had no part in it at all, as I never heard or saw any signs of his involvement. There were never to my knowledge any of the Guild people involved in any way with it. It was regarded, you might say, as one of the native sacred rites. I do not doubt for a moment, however, that Mr. Ashbee would have liked to have a hand in it in some way, but he probably shrank back in the realisation that it would not only look ridiculous, but be regarded as sacrilege. What one might say, though, is that he would have been anxious to inject new life and interest in Morris dancing and would probably have urged and encouraged it all he could, but that doesn't say he revived it. He certainly did all he could to revive the May Day revels. If there had been any such when we arrived they were apparently nothing to speak of, but the next May Day, 1903, the whole town was en fete. The maypole dance was revived, which I think had lain dormant for years[37].

The May Day festivities of that time were just for the local fun, not for the benefit of tourists with an eye on the 'box office'. That era was drawing to a close, although nobody knew it at the time. The same could be said of the Morris dances. The audience was a thin one with even thinner purses, so that any attempt at collecting money from them would probably have netted about threepence halfpenny.

- KC 22.4.82/10.7.82

May 1st: In Campden, as in all England even in London, it was a day of merrymaking, dressing up, clowning, singing and dancing. Even the horses had gay rosettes and ribbons.

These proceedings led up to the great moment, the crowning of the May Queen. There was a new one each year. The village maidens all lived in hopes of being picked, but I think the whole thing was one of simple beauty; it was all home made and sincere, clean and decent. Perhaps you may have read Tennyson's 'May Queen'. I can recall the following lines:

If you're waking call me early, call me early Mother dear
For tomorrow is the loveliest day of all the grand New Year
Of all the grand New Year, Mother, the maddest merriest day
For I'm to be Queen of the May, Mother,
I'm to be Queen of the May.

Have you ever seen the maypole dance? It dates back to medieval times. It takes a good bit of practice and drill to keep it from ending up in a fiasco of tangled ribbons. I do not know whether or not they still have any of it in Campden nowadays[38] ; it seemed a wonderful thing to me as a kid.

Nowadays Nature and all that goes with it is taken as a matter of course and perhaps often abused, but on May Day we used to dance and sing to it. Spring time in Gloucestershire was, and is today I guess, a beauteous sight.

Guy Fawkes Day was celebrated with fireworks and where possible, a bonfire where an effigy would be cast into the flames. Everyone had his own fireworks. In Campden there was a torchlight parade to the bonfire site and lots of fun and fireworks. I remember the schoolmaster, Mr. Dewey, one November 5th as we closed school that afternoon asking who had fireworks. Most had, but one or two poorest ones had no money to get any and he put his hand in his pocket and gave them money. Perhaps you have heard the old rhyme

"Please to remember the fifth of November
Gunpowder treason and plot.
I see no reason why gunpowder treason
Should ever be forgot."

As for Empire Day[39], it seemed to be more for children than grownups as I remember it. The schools marched to the square and sang a song or two in praise of the British Empire and raised and saluted the Union Jack. Actually it was the late Queen's birthday.

- CF 3.10.83

Viscount Campden's Coming of Age Celebrations: June 30-July 3, 1906

While on the subject of the Gainsboroughs, may I point out a paragraph in your book *[The Simple Life]* that I find somewhat distasteful as well as incorrect. Mr. Ashbee's views, on which you base it, seem to be coloured by intolerance and spite, surely unworthy of a man of culture and learning.

I think your reference to the Reverend Carrington as 'the Anglican parson, the hated Carrington who responded rather badly for the opposition God[40] ', if they were the words of Mr. Ashbee, were not worthy of publication in your book. Again, to quote: Mr. Ashbee 'could not resist pointing out that not a single labourer was anywhere in evidence, and - while not refusing the Earl's lavish hospitality - this led him to predict the inevitable doom for English aristocracy'[41] .

The facts are these, I remember them well as I was there. The festivities at Campden House lasted for three days. There were dinners and parties for all the notables for miles around. Our street, which was part of the route to Campden House, saw a procession of carriages coming and going during that time interspersed with a number of early motor cars popping and spluttering by. But when Mr. Ashbee says not a single labourer was in evidence, I am tempted to wonder if he was there at all, because in a field right in front of the House was a full sized roundabout or merry-go-round, several sets of swing boats and other fun of the fair attractions. This was all there for the duration of the festivities. All free. Come one, come all.

You could not miss hearing it, let alone seeing it. As you might expect, the place was thronged, not only by the village folk, but by many of the guests. While I was on the merry-go-round, who should come out but the Viscount himself with one or two friends. Room was made for them on board and we all went round together. You could have as many rides as you could get on.

Then on the last night of the festivities there was a dinner for all the

Gainsborough tenants which took care of most of the working class of the place. I don't suppose there was ever another such party there before or since. Incidentally, the Viscount served through World War One, but died at an early age leaving a six year old son who was the youngest Earl in England at the time[42] .

- FMc 5.9.81

People, Places, And The Odd Thought Or Two

About the church bells. They rang the curfew every night at 8 o'clock. There are eight bells and at that time (perhaps they still do) they rang a short tune like a small carillon every three hours in the daytime, at 3, 6, 9, 12 o'clock. I do not remember whether it was silent at night. One tune was the hymn 'Holy Holy Holy Lord God Almighty', another was 'The Bluebells of Scotland'. There were several others and they changed from time to time. Then of course if you heard the solemn tolling you knew that someone of more or less importance was dead. At weddings for $5 I mean £5 you could have the bell ringers on the job for a merry peal. I was married in Campden Church, but did not have the bells. I went back to England to marry a Campden girl and bring her here.

- CF 15.8.83

Talking of Campden Church. Yes, I must have spent quite a bit of time within it. My father was a regular attendant. Every Sunday morning without exception he would march us off with him to the morning service. For one thing it took us out of Mother's way while she cooked the Sunday dinner. My young brother Fred sang in the choir. We were sent to Sunday School in the afternoon, and at intervals the Sunday School paraded to the church for an afternoon service. This was the occasion one time for one of those 'once in a lifetime' happenings.

We had arrived in church and settled in the pews when I decided I would rather be in the next pew in front with a pal of mine. The shortest way there of course was over the back which I proceeded to follow, forgetting that I was right beside the teacher, an old gentleman, a baker and grocer; his shop was on the corner of High Street and Church Street by the Chestnut Tree[43]. I was halfway over the pew when he grabbed me by the tail of my jacket with his left hand and belaboured my head with the Bible he had in his right hand. It was one of those limp flexible ones and worked like a sandbag. He pulled me back in a half stupefied and docile condition. It isn't everyone who can say he was batted down in church.

- CF 14.4.84

1. Thatched Cottage, Watery Lane, Campden, about 1906
Herbert and Elizabeth Osborn, sons Fred, Bert and Harry

2. Campden National Schools Concert - Santa Claus Play, 1905
Standing, left to right: Gladys Curtis (Mrs. Reg. Smith),
Emily Keeley, Ernest Withers, Gertrude Willis, Edith Jesset.
Sitting: Harry Osborn, Anne Beavington, Harry Warmington (with 1st medal for Boys' School)

3. Henry Thomas Osborn about 1919

4. Chipping Campden Boys' School - about 1906

Mr. Dewey, Teacher

Harry Osborn, Back Row, 4th from left. Harry Warmington - Third Row, 1st left.

Bert & Fred Osborn - sitting together, right end of third row

5. Harry & Kathleen Osborn on their Wedding Day

6. Harry Osborn at his 90th Birthday Party

7. Maypole Dancing in Campden.
(Harry Osborn Kneeling in Front)

8. The Martins, High Street,
Home of Miss Freeman of the Penny Bank

9. C.R. Ashbee (1929)
by William Strang R.A.

10. Janet Ashbee
by William Strang R.A.

11. Alec Miller, Hilda Pook, George Chettle and F.L. Griggs

12. Swimming Gala at the Bathing Lake

13. Jim "Teapot" Williams

14. The Silk Mill, workshops of the Guild

15. The Visit of King Edward V11 to Campden, July 8 1905

16. H.W. Dolphin
a study by Alec Miller

17. Bob Dickinson

Our first house was in Sheep Street - No. 6 almost opposite to the Keytes and we became close friends. The father, old 'Napper' Keyte, was the main coal merchant of the place. There was a fair sized family, from grownups, like Garnet[44], to school age kids like myself, we played around together in their yard quite a lot. It was a big area, big enough to be occupied at times by travelling shows in big tents, like marionette shows and one time a menagerie of wild animals, lions, bears, wolves etc. All these travelling shows only stayed one night, so they never got a chance to associate socially with the people. The only exception was Holloway's, which, as I said before, stayed several months, and they may have had time for social calls, but it is doubtful. They must have had a busy time putting on a different show each night, six nights a week.

I knew Garnet Keyte well, he was a grown man and I often rode around with him on different vehicles and worked with him on his garden which was down near the station. Algy Hathaway[45] , too, was a familiar figure in those days, a merry fellow and well liked it seemed by all.

In Sheep Street I remember the entrance gate to the yard. There was a very old thatched cottage there on the right side of the gate as you go in. I used to sell bread there. The people were named Pinchin. The house was very old, almost crumbling into ruin and sunk into the ground as these old places seem to.

'Teapot' [46] was a well-known figure. I never knew his real name, perhaps he himself had forgotten it. He was always Teapot, grubbing a meagre living at odd jobs like scaring the birds out of cherry orchards and such like. After we left the house in Sheep Street, he lived in it with the people who occupied it. Whether he was related, I don't know, but he was always with them.

- CF 15.9.83/19.1.84

Sheep. There were very few in the fields adjoining Campden, except on market days in the Square. We used to see them dipped sometimes at the millpond at what was then Westington Mill at the end of Watery Lane. The mill pond has long since gone and the mill made into a large house. One thing I remember is lambs tails, they make a delectable dish when cooked. I remember going with my father over to Mickleton Hill farm early one morning. The Keytes who lived there were very nice and kindly people and we often visited them and had a good time. We were in time for breakfast and there was a large dish of baked lamb tails, their own of course. Lovable creatures, lambs, especially served up with mint sauce and new potatoes.

- CF 14.4.84

George Haines of Westington. He was known locally as Boss Haines and used to ride a horse whenever he came into Campden. That in itself is not unusual, all the farmers and everyone else from any distance did the same, but the horse Mr. Haines rode always seemed to go sideways prancing along broadside, so to speak. It took a long time to go a few yards. He never seemed to get it to follow its nose. George Hart married one of his daughters.

- CF 15.12.83

Kissing Alley was a portion of the footpath from Kingcombe Lane down to Campden. The path at this point ran between two thick hedges at the edge of one of the fields there. All those fields at that time were pasture. They had originally been cultivated for crops and the undulations of ridge and furrow were still plainly visible. The story was that they had ceased to be put into crop due to what has been known as the Corn Laws of the nineteenth century. Something about taxation, I suppose[47] .

The last time I saw it was in 1919 when I came through there with my wife-to-be. Then all those fields from Littleworth up to Kingcombe Lane were all grass and entirely devoid of buildings of any kind with the exception of an ancient thatched cart shed in Hoo Lane. (It was called Stoney Lane then). All there was in Littleworth was three old thatched cottages at the bottom corner at Back Ends.

- CF 25.10.83/15.12.83

As to the trees, elm and chestnut, they were not used as meeting places to my knowledge[48] ; their only claim to notice was that they were the only trees, other than those on private property, in Campden at that time. To be sure there were one or two small ones planted close to the sidewalk further up from the market hall, very insignificant scruffy little things which went unnoticed. The chestnut tree was a beautiful umbrella or mushroom shaft, you must have seen pictures of it. It had an iron seat all round it, a closed circle, which was often the haunt of a few old gaffers discussing their own ills as well as those of the world. The pump there also had no claim to importance in my time. The only time it ever made news was when a horse ran away dragging a cart and ran into it knocking it down and breaking off the urn-like top of it[49] .

- CF 15.12.83

I remember Mr. and Mrs. Trinder. He was a shoemaker (not just a shoe repairer) and he sometimes worked with Mr. Restall who was also a real shoemaker.

Mr. Restall was your *[A. W.'s]* grandmother Warmington's uncle. They lived in the house next door to what was then the Boy's School.

The Trinder House had something in common with two other houses in the High Street, one of which is the Post Office and the other one on the other side that juts out by the Market Hall. That is, that its upper storey is built with stone from the old mansion by the church that was burnt in the Civil War. Next time you go by, take a look and you will see what I mean. Sculpture does not belong on Cotswold houses, and the sculpture is exactly the same in each case. The ruins of the great house must have been a wonderful stone quarry[50].

- AW 9.6.79

I remember Mr. Taylor the photographer, also his daughter Dorothy, she would be in her late teens or older at that time. She used to teach piano in the elementary grade. Mr. Taylor of course had not the sophisticated stuff to work with. All his prints had to be on what was called 'daylight paper' which had to be exposed to daylight for hours at a time. I well remember the rows of little frames outside his shop, luckily it faced South. So-called 'gaslight paper' had only just been invented which of course speeded things up quite a bit.

- CF 19.1.84

The town crier in my time was real, not a showpiece[51]. He would be round whenever he had news to impart or to advertise something, as for instance, 'peapickers wanted on Mr. So and So's farm tomorrow morning, 6d per pot paid'. He had a handbell, probably the one used now, and would go to certain fixed spots around the town. It was 'Oyez, oyez, oyez' and would finish with 'God save the King'. It hadn't changed in centuries.

- CF 7.3.84

You ask where Heavenly Corner is, or was. For all I know it may have vanished without a trace by now, certainly if it is still there it must have been torn down and rebuilt as it was perhaps the most unappetising little slum in Campden. There were no more than three decrepit little cottages down there, though I was never bold enough to do more than look down it from its open end, it was a cul-de-sac. The enclosed little map will lead you to the spot if you wish to explore it.

The curious thing about the little tiny slums of Campden in those days, and there were more than Heavenly Corner, is that they all seem to have been hidden from the view of the passing visitor. They were entered down passageways between the High Street buildings, you can still see the passageways, but the wretched flea farm hovels have all been fumigated and done up or pulled down, at least I hope so. In the case of Heavenly Corner it was right behind several prestige houses.

- CF 13.7.84

The Guild of Handicraft

My duties in the office of the Guild were just those of the usual office boy first and foremost of which was to be, and to be regarded, as a general all round nuisance in the place. My proudest duty was to ring the bell to start and stop work. Here for a brief moment I was in command. The bell was a large long handled one similar to that of the town crier. At the appointed times I would step out of the office onto the platform you see in the pictures of the building and ring loud and long the command to start or stop. This bell could be heard over half of Campden and it had always been my ambition to perform on it.

Another duty was that of telephone operator. Yes we had our own telephone. There were five lines on it and the switchboard was in the outer office. One line was to Mr. Ashbee's office up the street, the others to the different shops in the building. Copying certain of the letters was another job at which I maintained my reputation of being a universal calamity. The letters were copied in a copying press which involved a damp cloth. Any time the cloth was a little too damp the original hand written letter would be smeared and of course had to be written again.

Mr.Webster *[the Office Manager]* was a very patient man, and a gentleman. I liked him very much. He must have had a feeling of relief when I left.

- FMc 17.6.81

C. R. Ashbee

I had never seen or heard of Mr. Ashbee at the period under discussion *[before 1902]*.[52] What I can say is, (if I may draw on my impression of later years) that you have drawn a fairly accurate picture of Mr. Ashbee as I knew him from my own observation and the opinions of the grownups around me. These always have a way of filtering down into the consciousness of an observant boy, so I offer the following remarks for what they are worth.

It has been said that each of us is three persons in one. First, as we see ourselves. Second as others see us. Third, as God sees us.

Leaving aside the third view, I would like to point out that the first view, in the case of Mr. Ashbee is mostly obtained from his own writings with some addition from Mrs. Ashbee.

I think the second view of any of us is the really important one of the two. What was the outside view of Mr.Ashbee? It varies with the viewer.

Mr. Ashbee was a genius./ Mr. Ashbee was a bit on the weird side.

Mr. Ashbee had a wide view./ Mr. Ashbee viewed the world through a crack in the fence.

Mr. Ashbee was a prophet./ Mr. Ashbee worshipped false gods. Opinion was divided among the guildsmen with, I always felt, the majority leaning to the second or negative one.

He had his own inner circle, it is true, but they were mere reflections of himself. Everybody of course paid him lip service, but in his absence he was spoken of with an amused smile.

His flock were not all that faithful to him or to his ideas; they were just out to earn a living, whether with handicraft in the country or in town with mass production. When better prospects presented themselves or the future began to look dim most were ready to take a better job.

This is not an attempt on my part to dim the picture of an admittedly remarkable man, but I put it forward as an absolute truth as the collective picture of him as seen by the workers, the fathers and mothers in his flock who only wished to live in the twentieth century, not with Mr. Ashbee in the sixteenth century.

- AC 4.3.1982

Of course, at that time I was just another grubby kid so I never had any personal communication to speak of, though I saw him quite often in the street striding along always looking straight ahead with head up with an air of being splendidly oblivious to everything below the clouds, as his thoughts always seemed to be up in the clouds.

He was always regarded with great respect, more than perhaps was given to his ideas behind his back. You refer to his book *Craftsmanship in Competitive Industry*. I also have a copy of it, but have never been able to make much out of it[53]. As I said though, I was just a boy and it is just my impressions at that age that you may be interested in, so I will try to keep it that way.

I have been present at lectures, purely adult affairs at which I will explain my presence later, where after the lecturer had finished and asked for any questions, Mr. Ashbee who was usually there would rise with a long winded question punctuated with many an 'er um, er so to speak' for several minutes and get so complicated that in the end he lost sight of his question and the audience were politely covering their smiles. The lecturer would thank him politely and turn to the next questioner.

I attended nearly all the plays, which all seemed to go off very well indeed. You have noted, I am sure, that they were all Elizabethan except 'The Rivals' by Sheridan. Mr. Ashbee loved to live in the past, his whole idea of the simple life belonged then. Instead of being advanced, his ideas were several centuries old which I think explains why they could not possibly work at a different period of history. Nevertheless his influence has affected so many of us down through the years in various ways that I feel we owe him a great debt. His three chief projects, I would say, were first the Guild and its move to Campden, then the Campden School of Arts and Crafts and next to that the bathing lake. None of them exist any more.

A year or two after our arrival Mr. Ashbee began his crusade to spread an appreciation of art among the natives by teaching it. His dream of a school to that end was only brought to reality after months of battling with the powers that be ensconced behind a rampart of red tape, but he finally succeeded and the Campden School of Arts and Crafts was born. There were classes in metalwork, carving, jewellery, etc. The teachers were no amateurs; they were the best of the guildsmen. My brother Bert joined the woodcarving class and in fact stayed with it for several seasons. The teacher here was no less than Alec Miller[54]. To me Alec Miller was the highest talented man of all the guildsmen. I saw much of his work and much of him doing it and it seemed no effort at all. Yet he was the quietest and most modest of all. I feel that he was the Mozart of wood carving, his talent seemed to gush out of him. The metalwork class had at least one pupil who made a lifetime of it as a silversmith. He was W.H.[*Harry*] Warmington, about a year younger than me. When the Guild broke up one of the silversmiths, J.Bailey, moved to Stratford-on-Avon and started on his own. W.H.W. went to work for him there; he showed sufficient talent that silversmithing became his life and work. Just as an aside here let me mention a couple of notable little items in connection. Mr. Bailey while at Stratford became the father of triplet boys, identical triplets all perfectly healthy. The papers made much of it locally at the time[55]. The other item is that his house in Stratford was next door to that of no less a person than Marie Corelli[56].

Well to get back on the track. W.H.W. eventually went back to Campden and worked for George Hart until he retired. For a time he used to commute to Gloucester to teach there. He was reputed in certain circles to be one of the finest silversmiths in the country. I know he was presented to the Queen and Princess Elizabeth at some exhibition of the craft. I know all this because I married his sister.

- FMc 17.6.1982

The School of Arts and Crafts,[57] more easily spoken of as the Technical School or Tech for short, was one of the great binding influences in Campden.

Hitherto there had been no, or very little chance of obtaining practical knowledge of the crafts that were now offered. Moreover, the fees were negligible, 2/6 for the season. There was something going on all the time. The lecture room was also ideal for band practice, and under Mr. Pyment we had a first class band. The carving class was very popular under Alec Miller, there were ladies as well as gents in it. It always seemed to me to be one of the most convenient arts as well as pleasant and rewarding. The outlay for tools was small and with a piece of wood and a table you could practice at home if you wished. The same workshop also doubled as a carpenter's or cabinet maker's. The same benches, but different tools and teacher. The boy's school which I attended had one or two extracurriculum classes, one of which was woodwork, (not carving) and a group of us were chosen to attend that once a week on Friday afternoon. This took place in the workshop above mentioned with a guildsman, Mr. Wall, as teacher.

There was a gardening class, of which you have a picture[58]. Bert was in that. Our school also had a gardening class along the same lines. I belonged to that. There was a swimming class after the Bathing Lake was finished, both at the Tech and at our school. Until the advent of the Tech none of this existed, so it had a far reaching effect on both the young and the grown ups.

I have already mentioned the metal working class. There was Cookery. This was also a free class from the girls' school. The equipment may have been a bit primitive alongside present day stuff, but perhaps it was more in keeping with the simple life. The whole thing seemed in a way to affect nearly everyone; either you belonged to a class or someone in the family or close friend did, so it seemed to connect most of the town together.

Nowadays I suppose opportunities for education and training are so many that it is all taken for granted, but at that time in Campden and hundreds of similar places there was nothing.

- FMc 5.9.81

The bathing lake was an innovation. It was the first time in the history of the place a piece, or body, of water was available for swimming. The only standing water hitherto had been mill ponds which were private property and taboo for bathing.[59]

I don't know whether the idea was wholly Mr.Ashbee's but he was no doubt the motive power. As far as I know it was all dug out by hand. I used to get a look at it under construction after hours when nobody was around. (You had to cross private property to reach it). I never saw any earth moving machinery so it appears to have been just pick and shovel. It was filled by the brook, a sluice gate at each end, but it was not lined, just earth sides and bottom like a natural swimming hole in a river. The enclosed badly packed pictures may give a little idea of it. Note the curtained dressing rooms. It doesn't exist now. I understand there is a swimming pool at Broad Campden to take its place, probably a bit more sophisticated.[60]

The old bathing lake was not in the town; it was perhaps a third of a mile out and the only approach was through farm land which was only open to the public during the hours when the pool was open. From time to time there were gala days there, with all sorts of competitions, races, diving, polo games, etc., and even comedy acting on the far bank. I remember one involving an innocent swimmer who left his clothes on the ground while he went for a swim. Along came an escaped convict in prison garb who proceeded to change clothes. This of course led to a struggle with much falling into the water fully clothed, producing shrieks of delight from the audience. The end was predictable. The convict ran away in the other's clothes. The innocent man put on the prison garb, a policeman came along and arrested him as the escaped convict, and they all ended up in the water once more, to the delight of the crowd over the policeman's ducking.

Ah, 'Them was the days'!

- FMc 17.6.81

Janet Ashbee

Mrs. Ashbee was one of the finest persons I ever knew. Even today after all these years her very memory generates a feeling of warmth in me, which cannot be expressed in words. She seemed to me to carry with her an invisible aura of love, or friendship, or whatever it was, that was serenely lovely and rare.

One always felt comfortable in her presence. She could bring herself down to whatever level you were and you would find yourself trying to reach hers. She often came to our house, which is something Mr. Ashbee never did. Apart from his inner circle I don't remember him visiting the homes of any of the men. But Mrs. Ashbee was always eager for the company of others. One of her joys, which is mentioned in your book *[The Simple Life]*, was to gather round her a small group of children of age about 10 or over and lead the troop, like the Pied Piper, across the fields and down lanes teaching us songs as we went along. We would sit in a circle round her for a rest, perhaps 2 or 3 miles from home and have a debate on something or other, sing, ask riddles and what not. At those times, this great lady was one of us. There were carol singers, groups of kids going from door to door looking for a penny or two. Mrs. Ashbee went a step further. For two years in succession she organised a carol singing group. This consisted of about 12 or 14 boys and girls. She had us in her drawing room teaching a repertoire of carols we had never heard before. She spent many hours at the piano trying to get us to sound more like skylarks than the flock of crows we were. When the time drew nigh for us to go into action she had red cloaks and hoods made for us all, which perhaps made us look better than we sounded. A few nights before Christmas she issued forth with us in marching order out for business. She knew just where to go to perform. Anybody known to be thin of pursc, we didn't waste time on. After the evening's exertions we marched back to Woolstapler's Hall where we were regaled with hot cocoa and cakes served by a uniformed, white aproned parlour maid. Several nights of this till Christmas. I think this is one of the most treasured memories of Mrs. Ashbee that I have[61].

What I have just said about not stopping at poor people's doors was not by any means, other than a desire to refrain from recovering from them what they could not spare.

Mrs. Ashbee was much interested in *[my crippled elder brother]* Bert and could see that he had in hands and mind the potentialities of a good craftsman, and encouraged it in every way. He studied wood carving and metal work and leather work and became quite proficient at it later. She knew many people in London and procured orders from them for various handcrafted articles. This was an immense encouragement for him, as it overcame any feeling of hopeless uselessness he may have had. Being a student at the School of Arts and Crafts automatically admitted him to the lectures, not that he attended many of them, but I was out in the cold as it were as I was not a student, but I did want to get in and hear what was going on.

Mother must have mentioned it to Mrs. Ashbee, who called and questioned me about it, as to whether I had tried to get in. I had, and had been thrown out. That was enough for Mrs. Ashbee. She called for pen and paper and wrote out a pass to the effect that this would admit me to any lectures I wished to attend, nem. con., and signed by herself. I knew what the nem. con. meant and proudly marched up to the door and flashed it under the doorman's nose. He started to question me and I casually pointed out 'nem. con.' and passed in.

I attended many lectures there, not that I understood some of them, but I suppose I derived a feeling of importance which partly made up for it. Mrs. Ashbee senior also paid us a visit or two, in company of her daughter-in-law when she came to Campden. To illustrate the interest Mrs. Ashbee showed in Bert I will mention this instance. One day she arrived with some small wooden furniture suitable for a doll's house, a dining room chair and table, etc. The chair stood about four inches high to the top of the back, and the rest in proportion. These were to be samples, if Bert thought he could make them to order. Mrs. Ashbee would get the orders. They were made of cigar box wood. Mrs. Ashbee would see about a supply of that. Consequently father got the tools and whatever was needed such as glue and fine nails. The parts had to be cut out with a fret saw and put together, nailed and glued so that the pieces were quite sturdy and solid when finished. Bert was in business from that moment and Mrs.

Ashbee was shipping sets of these things to London and bringing more orders. Cigar boxes were coming in as fast as the goods were going out, even a good sized bale of them from London one day. The labels of course had to be removed, but the wood in those days was lovely to work. I wonder today if any of that miniature furniture still exists.

I am very proud to have known this great lady. One of her activities was a series of lectures on songs of the past, from the seventeenth and eighteenth centuries. The lectures were sandwiched in among the other lectures. She would rope in some tenor or soprano friend to illustrate, while she accompanied at the piano. She roped in myself and three other boys to sing at one of them. It took much rehearsing to get us into shape, and I have always had the feeling that she winced inwardly at our efforts.

- FMc 5.9.81

Guild People

Mr. Ashbee's office was in an upstairs room in the High Street just opposite the end of Sheep Street. He had, as you know, a private secretary in the person of Miss Pook. She was an attractive young lady, well liked and respected by all. Always well and smartly dressed and very pleasant in manner. She had the most jaunty walk, though, bobbing up and down at every step. I used to think that she and Mrs. Ashbee in the matter of dress and carriage were the two most lovely women in Campden, like two swans in a flock of turkeys. She eventually married Ron Haydon, as you know, but that was after we left. Ron Haydon was well liked, but always seemed a very quiet, sedate person. He was a farmer's son and she a lady with much sparkle, almost opposites you might say, but perhaps when she got him alone you would be surprised. I remember her particularly as being the teacher of a short lived class of shorthand and typing.

When I first assumed my duties in the office of the Guild the manager, Mr. Webster, asked me if I would like to learn shorthand and typing, as a class was being started. He would finance it, so I was duly enrolled. Mr. Vickery, the senior clerk, also joined. I was the youngest one. The rest were all males in late teens or thereabouts. The outcome was not surprising. Nobody took it seriously in Miss Pook's presence. Much more attention was paid to the teacher than to her teaching and after a few sessions the class was no more.

- FMc 17.6.81

Ted Horwood was a guildsman and lived in the house behind the elm tree, next door to the baker's where I worked. I forget what he did at the Guild[62], but he was a good photographer and spent much time at it, just as a hobby as far as I know. In World War One he was in the Royal Flying Corps as an aerial photographer over the lines. That of course was in its infancy then. I met him after the war and he said it was like a tonic to him and he was sorry it was all over.

- CF 7.3.84

I knew Thomas Binning[63] well. He lived next door but one to us. He was quite a refined old gentleman, a widower with one daughter and a housekeeper. Myself and brothers and sometimes another boy would go and visit him, which I think pleased him. He would gather us around him and talk to us in a way that we found full of interest as he seemed to be very well read. We always regarded him as a kind of friend and gentleman. His daughter Millie worked in the Guild as a bookbinder.

Walter Curtis[64] was another well respected person in our eyes. He and his wife were very staid and upright people. Typical Victorians in outlook and family life. Their daughter (Gladys) married a Campden man, one of the leading men in Campden, R.R. Smith. Her son is now Mayor of Campden[65].

- AC 4.3.82

Miss Power[66] . She always seemed to be referred to as Miss Power or Ann Power. I never heard the name Statia. She was rather a masculine type and used to stride about like a man, long swinging strides. She was regarded generally as something of an Amazon. She eventually got married and the quip was going around that she had 'resigned from Power'. She lived in the house, or rather one of the houses, in that island of houses in the High Street.

- FMc 1.9.81

The Craftsman's Club

The Craftsman's Club. Now that is something that comes close to home, our home.

I am not sure just who advanced the first idea of it, but my father seemed to have been the backbone of it. It was, as far as I recall, strictly a recreation club. There was a bar and all that goes with it, a billiards room, facilities for all sorts of indoor recreation.

Father was secretary, treasurer, purchasing agent, in fact he seems to have carried the whole burden of it on his back. He did this from its inauguration until we left Campden. I don't think it survived very long after that. But it was a jolly old thing while it lasted. It took up father's evenings, sometimes six days a week. It got that when he wasn't there he was working on the office work. He had the small bedroom in our house fixed up for an office.

Mother was not amused, but fortunately she only protested mildly. Father was a non-drinker and a very faithful servant to the club. It could have been worse. I was not involved in it. It was strictly adult. The building was one of the Island houses. Miss Power's house backed on to it. I do not doubt it was an interesting establishment and probably had many an interesting visitor, as many such came to Campden and were probably invited to the club. The wives and families were invited once. That was the occasion of the debut of a large new gramophone of a loudness never heard in Campden before. That was the only time I think I was ever inside. Mother was given the honour when the club started of making the red window blinds. Later on I was entrusted with the position of paymaster, in that father sent me forth with the money to pay the local merchants once a month. I used to usually get a handout of sweets or cakes or something of the kind from various shops.

- FMc 1.9.81

It took up most of his time, but I am quite sure it was an unpaid job. He was the kind of man who would feel dishonest if he accepted any reward for something he enjoyed doing. For instance, as you are aware, there are big profits in the brewing and distilling industries and they were always generous to anyone connected with their sales come Christmas. Whenever this was offered to father in his capacity as purchasing agent he steadfastly refused it as bribery. He told me this himself. The agent who offered it probably pocketed it himself.

Perhaps this is irrelevant to Mr. Ashbee and the Guild, but it is a sidelight on the Craftsmen's Club. I don't know of any public service they engaged in, it seemed to be more of a refuge and sanctuary than anything. Whether Mr. Ashbee went there I cannot say. I never heard my father mention it.

- FMc 5.9.81

The End of the Guild

It must soon have been evident that after the move it was starting to wither, like a plant that is transplanted sometimes withers and dies. This, I think, was felt by my uncle W.J. Osborn. Anyhow he resigned in 1905 only three years after the move, having been with the firm for many years in London[67]. He returned to London and from there to Maidstone in Kent where he spent the rest of his active life teaching for the Kent Education Committee. He was a first-rate cabinet maker.

I remember him taking me one evening after hours, sometime before he left, or perhaps thought of leaving, into a large room on the ground floor of the Guild which was kept locked. It was perhaps 30' x 30' say 900 square feet. This was full of finished work all unsold. Here were beautiful cabinets, writing desks, sideboards, etc.; wrought-iron articles, copper pieces. All this had been made for stock to keep men employed. This of course was not the fault of WJO. He had to follow the instructions from above.

To ship it to London would cost money enough to wipe out the profit. There was the disadvantage of being so far from the market, plus the number of non-producers on the payroll.

Looking back now it seems that the Guild never got off the ground at any time after the move. It was, as it were, living on itself.

If there was any feeling of depression or panic during the last months I cannot say. Little of it was apparent to me at home, as things of moment such as this were not discussed in the hearing of us kids, and I wasn't in the office long enough to know what the normal amount of business should be. When we did have to move back to London it was with mixed feelings. We loved the old house and garden and the country all around it, but for me at least it held the promise of learning a trade, hopefully that of a machinist.

My time in the office, short as it was, was not wasted. I learned in that time that I was not made for office work.

- FMc 17.6.81

III

AFTER CAMPDEN

London

On our return in December 1907 we found some changes in the street traffic, for one thing. When we left in 1902 the streets were full of horsedrawn traffic, buses, tram cars, cabs, carts, fire engines, etc., but now there were to be seen in some places motor buses, electric trams, a few motor cars all mixed up with horse traffic, but apart from that the general economic condition had not altered perceptibly.

Unemployment was rife and there was no 'dole', so there was a lot of distress and hunger among the working class. This, of course, was the case all over the country. Outside the doors of factories it was quite the usual thing to find a small crowd of old men and children also, waiting for the workers at quitting time to give them any remains of their lunch. You didn't throw any food away, there were always hungry ones waiting for it, almost fighting over it. It was no uncommon sight to see old men in a crowd of boys all applying for a boy's job at, of course, boy's wages.

I found myself in the middle of this on starting back in London. I started with a job at a famous surgical instrument makers with high hopes, but the apprentices there were indentured and us boys strictly on the outside, there was no chance. Other places followed in other shops, but it became apparent it was leading nowhere. I took up other work to keep going and eventually we decided to try somewhere else and came to Canada in 1914.
- CF 14.4.84

When we left Campden, things were not rosy. My father's trade was a dead one. He had followed his father's trade, that of an ivory worker, but that had all gone out of fashion and died when I was very young. His work at the Guild was not with ivory. My grandfather must have been a first class artist of it. I have seen much of his work, and I have a set of ivory chess men of his making, a beautifully detailed piece of work. All this by the way. My father's health was getting poor, the dust from wood turning made it impossible to follow that trade anymore, so from then on his income was, to say the least, precarious. I was thirteen and a half at that time. My ambition was to be apprenticed to the engineering trade, but there was no chance of an indentured apprenticeship without money. I had jobs in machine shops but nothing with any future in them. The real apprentices were the sacred cows, the rest of us were not much better than errand boys. What I am trying to say is, if you wanted to eat in those days you had to work hard for it. I worked in one shop from 6.30 a.m. till 5.30 p.m. and Saturday morning for 5/- a week. A boy's wages at that time were about 6/- to 7/- a week. Everyone nowadays seems to have money to spend and I suppose when you can get money without working for it, or at least working but little, it is just human nature to lay off. It is the same here *[in Canada]* and I am sure in the U.S. also. Farms that I knew in my early days here that were once bustling hives of industry with parents and kids all eagerly at work, are now idle and empty. The kids have grown up and gone to town. Health services in those days, however, did not seem too bad. In Campden Dr. Dewhurst charged 1/- for a visit; but there was no hospital closer than Shipston, if there. People only had a doctor when they really needed it. Nowadays everyone seems to be flocking to get checkups, needles, shots and drugs of all kinds.

In London, doctors charged 6d, that is, among the poor. One Dr. I remember only charged 3d. He was known as the 'threepenny doctor'. I don't know how good he was. The main hospitals in London were free. They were supported by all sorts of voluntary contributions, tag days, rose days, etc. Rose Day was Queen Alexandra's birthday. She was the Queen Mother of her day, beloved of everyone, Edward VII's wife. Everyone bought and wore roses, like poppies on Armistice. Patients who had received treatment, on their discharge were given a kind of sheet of stamps to sell amongst friends and send in the money. I wonder if they still do that.

- CF 7.3.1984

Canada

The Merrimans lived opposite us in Watery Lane (Pardon me. Park Rd). As a lad Wilfred Merriman had worked at Campden House for a while and then in the office at the Guild. From there to London a few months before we moved back there. Then (he was in domestic service) the people paid his way to Canada to an Agricultural College. We only heard from him once in a blue moon. At this time, 1913, my younger brother Fred who was employed in office work, developed lung trouble and after hospital treatment etc. was pronounced fit again, but warned by the Dr never to do inside work again. "Go to sea. Join the Navy or Merchant Marine, anything like that". Well, the Navy turned him down. The Merchant Marine was full up. What to do? Just then a letter arrived from Canada from Wilf Merriman and from that things took a natural course. Fred went to join 'Bill' in Canada, who had left college and was working around farms and lumber camps on his own.

We all packed up and came here in 1914.

World War I started in Aug. Bill was one of the first to join. Fred joined up a little later. Bill went right through the war and came back and lived at my parents' home almost as a member of the family until he got married. Fred never came back. Bill died in 1942.

- AW 9.6.1979

Thoughts and Memories.

Let me tell you the case of my own mother, this was during World War 1[68]. We were here in Canada living away in the backwoods in Quebec Province in almost complete isolation. My father and I were working in Ottawa not able to go home very often, so that there was only Mother and my elder brother Bert, who was crippled. My younger brother Fred was overseas at the war. One night, Mother woke and heard somebody call her. 'Mum'. She thought it was Bert, in the next room, and hurried to see what was the matter, but he was sleeping soundly and was never known to talk in his sleep. It was not until word came a few days later that Fred was killed and she found it coincided with the date and approx time of Fred's death.

Much of the same happened to me when my wife died. She was in the hospital. I am a fitful sleeper sometimes and on this night I awoke for a few minutes and heard a call from her bedroom next to mine. She always called me 'Pop'. I heard this call and started up to see what she wanted and suddenly remembered she wasn't there. The call came again much fainter. I looked at the time, 2.10 a.m. It was about 4 a.m. when the phone rang from the hospital to say she had passed away in her sleep, the time it had happened would be about the time I heard the call.

- CF 3.10.1983

Many years ago I was working as a machinist in a small factory *[in Canada]*. The foreman was a small man who was married the day after I was and they lived only around the corner from us, we knew them pretty well, in fact I knew his mother and the rest of the family. Their first baby was a boy named Lloyd (after Lloyd George). You might say it was quite a very ordinary set up, duplicated millions of times down through history, just poorly educated working people. However, the baby Lloyd had a fairy godmother. He showed such signs of promise that his parents provided him with a university education, and I don't think he ever looked back. To give a list of the important positions he has held would be out of place here, but he has been returned to Parliament several times, where he now is. A year or so back he was named Deputy Speaker, and now is made Speaker, to take effect in a few days, when the present Speaker, a lady, is to be made Governor General of Canada. So the Speaker will be Lloyd Francis, whom I have known from birth. He has visited at this house, not as a politician but as a personal friend. I get a card from him every Christmas[69].

- AW 9.1.84

IV

POSTSCRIPT: A GOOD STORY

King Edward VII visits Campden

The thoughts and memories of the preceding pages have been cut and pasted from more than a score of Mr. Osborn's letters. The following is a single letter, written to Col. Geoffrey Powell about a detail in Col. Powell's Book of Campden *with which Mr. Osborn took exception. The result is a long and wonderful story about turn-of-the-century Campden. This letter tells us, more than any other, what a fine storyteller we lost in Mr. Osborn's passing.*

426 Leighton Terrace
Ottawa
Apr 5 83

Col. Geoffrey Powell

Dear Sir,

In hope that you still remember me, and at the risk of being associated with the many useless and unavoidable nuisances of life, may I rise to speak with regard to your 'Book of Campden'. I am sure we both have a sufficiently deep interest in Campden history to gather up any crumbs of it we find, so anything I have to say is offered only in the desire for accuracy as far as can be discovered and not in any way a criticism of your work. With that end in view let me offer the following:

On page 93 you show a picture of the King's car passing through Campden, also a picture of Bob Dickinson, who should forever be associated with that event.

First I wish to point out that the date is wrong wherever you obtained it. Christopher Whitfield has it wrong also[70] . Perhaps that is where you got it, which shows how often history can be distorted and corrupted when errors get handed down.

The actual date was 1906[71] . How do I know? Because I was there. We had left Campden by the end of 1907. This, however is not the reason for my writing, the date is immaterial, but what seems to me to be regrettable is the dimming and eventual loss of a good story by the glossing over or publishing such condensed or erroneous accounts as you give in nothing more than a few words in a caption of a picture. True, the matter was nothing more than a slightly ludicrous happening, smacking perhaps of P.G. Wodehouse or even Gilbert and Sullivan, but if Campden has the tragedy of The Campden Wonder to hug to its breast, I feel that the story of Bob Dickinson and His Majesty King Edward VII deserves better preservation than it has so far received.

In all the history of Campden with the visits of reigning monarchs few and far between, where will you find anything so audacious as this or a monarch so good-humouredly entering into the joke as accepting a gift from a mendicant who stops his car in mid journey on a Sunday afternoon. The crowned head of the mighty British Empire, Emperor of India, Fid Def and all, graciously accepted the paper and continued his progress.

The Campden Wonder has been presented in book form and on the stage. (I have seen it there myself). Why should this little moment of comedy with the King and the royal arms be relegated to half a dozen words under a picture?

May I therefore offer you a first hand account of the matter as I am perhaps one of the very few persons living who can give the story first hand.

To understand what seems to me to be vital to the joke it is necessary to introduce another very interesting character. He was known only as Dolphin as far as I ever knew. Campden at that time had a roster of unusual characters ranging from the mere eccentric down through the grades to the village idiot. Dolphin was fairly well up on the list. He had been a postman in his day and still considered himself a Govt official. He still had his postman's hat as well as the overcoat, both of which he always wore. The coat was one of several which he usually had on at the same time, the longest one on first so that you could always count them.

Around this wardrobe he wore a red white and blue belt with a snake fastener, and tucked into the belt he usually in season had a collection of buttercups, daisies, or whatever flowers he could gather for his decoration of himself.

He also had a watch chain visible at times which bore a generous collection of hardware such as door keys and a little toy shovel of cast iron, a child's toy about four inches long.

He lived alone in a house on the top side facing the Red Lion. Here in the window you could, if so inclined, stop and read his poems; the window was full of such things, with sometimes children's drawings which he had come by. It was the literary centre of Campden. Sometimes he pulled down the blind which was made of a green banner on which in large letters was displayed those noble words -

God Bless Our Queen

In his younger days he appears to have been a person of perhaps fairly high intellect with the mind of a gentleman, at least he appeared so to me. I don't think he drank nor did I ever hear him use bad language, but he was very active, a veritable busybody at times. Sometimes he would stand outside his house on the bank reading out his latest prose or poetry to a circle of open mouthed children and a few of the village oafs.

In build he was of medium height, grey whiskered and somewhat bent with age. Whether he ever got all his raiment off is hard to say; it would take long to get it all on again. I think he got a handout from the butchers once in a while.

I remember my father telling me that he had passed Dolphin's house one day and saw the old man out on the pavement with a saucepan and half a sheep's head. The sheep's head was a little too tight to go right into the saucepan so Dolphin had the saucepan on the ground and was stamping the head in with the heel of his boot.

This then is a thumbnail sketch of Dolphin.

The story begins on a Sunday afternoon. We were all seated at midday Sunday dinner at about 1 p.m. Hurried steps were heard approaching our door and a loud knocking followed. Dolphin was at the door in great excitement. "King be a coming, two o' clock" he panted out and repeated it as he hurried off to the next house with his tidings. He aroused everyone in the street.

We didn't know what to make of it for a time, after all poor old Dolphin had probably got some story mixed up and was not to be relied on.

When we became aware that the rest of the neighbors were all wending their way 'down town' we thought we might as well follow the crowd and had not long to wait, for at about 2 p.m. the royal car came down Sheep St. and turned up High St. I had a very good view of the King, within three feet it seemed, then he was gone and that was that, or so we thought. My father told me the following some time after.

He and Supt. Jones were fairly close friends and in conversation the Supt. related how he had been notified by those responsible for the King's movements that His Majesty would pass through Campden in Lord Redesdale's car en route for Batsford Park at 2 p.m. approx. The Supt. then called his force together, which consisted of a sergeant and one constable and ordered them to see that no untoward incident occurred to interfere with the king's journey. 'Above all things' he said, 'keep your eye on Dolphin. Don't let him out of your reach'.

So while the Campden Police Force were keeping at Dolphin's elbow, here was Bob Dickinson calmly standing in the road near Broad Campden to stop the royal vehicle, handing in the paper with probably a humble bow, and the king accepting both with a smile and driving on. This, it always seems to me is part of the point of the joke, the police ready to grab Dolphin while the villain of the piece is at work.

Nothing more was thought of it at the moment, few knew anything of the incident until several weeks later, when Bob Dickinson strutted out on his Sunday route flashing a brand new bag bearing the Royal Arms.

According to Christopher Whitfield p.249 he ... "stopped the car and insisted on selling the King a paper- after which he painted a version of the Royal Arms on his canvas bag and claimed to be a purveyor to Royalty; a distinction upon which he insisted, to the amusement of visitors for many a year after."

To say that he insisted on *selling* a paper to the king is childishly absurd. There were three other men in the car beside the king, Lord Redesdale[72] and two in the front seat, who could and would have dealt with anybody insisting on anything with His Majesty. Dickinson was too wary a bird not to know that. He evidently, as the car halted proffered a paper through the open window of the car, which the king, sportsman that he was, accepted.

Dickinson was not a native of Campden, he was from Birmingham and sounded like it. So much for hearsay or history. The facts are that when the incident was made known to the publishers in London they quickly recognized it as a good story and must have contacted Buckingham Palace for confirmation. The result evidently was that the king enjoyed the affair and granted permission for the use of the royal arms. Had this not been so, it is without doubt that the use of the arms would have been quickly suppressed, not only by the proper authorities but by the publishers themselves. I have no doubt too that Supt. Jones would have loved to have a hand in it as well. I saw this bag many times, it came to our house every Sunday, a beautiful piece of work, royal blue and gold done by an expert hand. When this got shabby a new one appeared, evidently from the publishers. Toward the end of his active life it was changed to an engraved brass plate, but if you would like confirmation on that, I suggest you might talk to Mrs. Frank James. She lives next door to Cutts' Garage.

That is all I have to say at this time. I offer the foregoing just as a passing thought in the hope that perhaps the story will be of interest to you, even if it is just a brief glimpse of Campden in the last years of its natural glory, the end of an era which was to outlast the king who had just passed through but a few short years.

I shall be glad to hear from you any time.

Until then, with all good wishes

Yours very truly

H.T. Osborn

FOOTNOTES

[1]factory floor. Mr. Osborn was a child when the Guild moved to Campden, and although he had a taste of the competitive workplace after (as he tells us), he can't convey the experience of an adult workman discovering the Guild after having worked elsewhere. The following is an extract from a letter of condolence to Janet Ashbee upon the death of her husband C.R. Ashbee in 1942. The letter was written by a Guildsman who believed deeply in the Guild, and carried it with him for the rest of his life, but had to leave Campden when the business broke up. He went to work at Cadbury's in Birmingham, working on new moulds for chocolate. He named his house "Campden", kept up his own silversmithing, and occasionally lectured and taught silversmithing.

> "...at thirteen years of age I was pitchforked into industry to pick up scraps of knowledge the best way I could for even then the apprentice system had gone. My entrance was like thousands of others, just chucked down the warehouse steps into one of those black holes in a back street, with the remark 'This is the kid to sweep up and do errands'; in this firm, calling themselves Gold and Silversmiths, and for the magnificent sum of five shillings per week I cleaned, made tea, fetched beer and often things I could not get, like strap oil, or to the little shop for Pigeon Milk; and very often filling in dirty little bits of paper with horses or football teams ready for the threepenny or sixpenny bet, and I might say at the expense of my dinner coppers I often had, and flatter myself my Mother having four of us to clothe and feed on her earnings as a dressmaker you can guess her only interest was my wage packet.
>
> Now, if one understands the environment of these shops, with their four-holed tables, and three-legged stools and twenty or thirty men sitting around in a room not much bigger than a sitting room, these places are inducive to conversation and chaff, because, except for the click of tweezers or the burr of the blow pipe; (for the noise

of the hammer has gone, because most of the smithing is stamped or spun on the machines in other places). The conversation settled Empires, picked the best footballers, destroyed the Boss, whom they don't respect because they know him. Not like his father. And workmen's smutty tales from the wag who deals in them; and the sex problem comes at one from the tales of how long the insurance or gas man was in one of the next door houses, or what the boss and the office girl are up to. Then comes the ambition to get put on the bench. One of the men offers to take you on, because he can earn more on some repetition job but after a bit begins to get afraid of his own job because the youth gets too wise or fashions change. It ended in 'the sack': to cut a long story short, I went on in this chaos always hating my work, reading the romance of Cellini and his work; of Morris in his talks of the Joy of Labour, when, as a young married man by accident I heard of C.R. Ashbee with his Guild of Art Workers was moving from the East End of London to Chipping Campden, I asked leave to join, and from the minute I walked down the beautiful sleepy street of Campden and under the influence of C.R.A. and others who I found (under his direction) were turning out work equal to anything in the middle ages. Industry meant something different, and from that time I have enjoyed every minute of my workday life."

It is signed "Walter Edwards, M.R.A., Craftsman", and was written when he was past seventy. I have taken this directly from a typed copy of the letter, in the possession of Felicity Ashbee, at the bottom of which Janet Ashbee has written: "I had this typed as almost illegible in original."

[2] Gas street lighting. Gas and gas lighting first came to Campden in 1870. The Guild brought electricity into the Silk Mill using their own generator, but mains electricity didn't reach Campden until 1928. There was a first experiment in electric street lighting in 1934, when the Shropshire, Worcestershire and Staffordshire Electric Power Company proposed the installation of 42 lamps - three more than were lit by gas. The town later reverted to gas and in 1960 there was an initiative to change back from gas to electric lighting in the High Street. A parish meeting vetoed this on aesthetic grounds, but in 1965 the Town Council took the decision to have the High Street lamps electrified.

[3] Metropolitan Railway. The world's first underground railway opened between Farringdon Street and Paddington Station in 1863.

[4] Boer War (1899-1902). The South African War, in which Britain extended its rule over the Afrikaner Transvaal. Five Campden men died in the war, and four old boys from the Grammar School. At one point, according to the town doctor, there were forty-six or forty-seven Campden men serving in the war, and in a claim later echoed by Canon Bourne of Weston Subedge, he said "Campden occupied a unique place in the United Kingdom, in that it sent out more men in proportion to its population than any other town" *(Ev J*, 16.6.1900, *Ev J* 8.12.1900). Compare these numbers with the sixty that were killed from Campden in the First World War.

[5] Elysian Fields. In Greek Mythology, the equivalent of Paradise or Heaven.

[6] Mr. Pyment. James W. Pyment, elected a Guildsman in 1894, became leader of the Town Band soon after arriving in Campden, and led it to victory in the 9th annual Madresfield Musical Competitions in 1904. When the Guild collapsed, he remained in Campden at the head of his own company of builders and ecclesiastical wood-workers. He bought the Silk Mill premises when the Guild Trust folded during World War One, and leased the workshops to the Guildsmen still at work in them. Both Pyment's Builders, and Hart's Silversmiths, of the original workshops, are still housed in the Silk Mill.

[7] One and a half butcher's shops. According to the *Kelly's Directory* published in 1902, Campden had three butchers: Herbert Baylis, W.H. Coldicott and Sons, and Edwin Ladbrook. All three were listed again in the 1906 edition. Ladbrook was a pork butcher and perhaps this is Mr. Osborn's "half". The 1902 and 1906 *Kelly's Directories* list three, rather than two, grocers in Campden, although their sizes are not indicated. In 1902 they were T. W. Coleman and Sons, of Banbury; John Hobbs; and Herbert Wixey. Hobbs - a grocer/baker - was replaced in the 1906 edition by Henry J. Hands, chemist/grocer. The drapers were Julius Neve (also the postmaster) and Roberts and Co. According to Mr. Don Ellis, their stocks were suited to local tastes, but materials suited to London tastes could be ordered by using sample books.

[8] Women. It was only later that C.R. Ashbee recognised the necessity of taking wives into account. In the introduction to part IV of his *Memoirs* (p.285 of the King's College, Cambridge, version), written in 1938, Ashbee says: "...the woman, - the wife of the craftsman - determines his life and shapes his character in ways you would never imagine and that however well your plans may be laid she may upset them. That is what 'woman's

suffrage' really means. In other words evolution and culture among men can only get to a certain point. Unless you develop the woman too, he can get no further. The idea behind the Guild has to be looked at then in the light of these two human discoveries."

[9] Shinkicking. One of the famous Cotswold sports, played to within living memory. Men with metal-toed boots would kick each others' shins, having first toughened their own by hitting them with boards or hammers, and treating them with home-made embrocations. The scars remained for life.

[10] Campden House. Not old Campden House, which was burned during the Civil War, and the remains of which can still be seen near the Church. New Campden House, also called Coombe Manor at the end of the last century, was rebuilt for Viscount Campden early in the 19th century, and stands on extensive grounds outside of Campden towards Broadway.

[11] Martin-Holland. Robert Holland-Martin (1872-1944), a director and later chairman of Martin's Bank, London, who resided at Overbury Court in nearby Overbury, Worcs. He became interested in the Guild in 1897, and thereafter was one of its closest friends and financial advisors. He was made an honorary Guildsman in 1898, and played a key role in finding and helping the Guild to settle in Campden.

[12] Kitchener stove. That is, a proper kitchen stove, rather than the open fireplace Mrs. Osborn had used for cooking in Sheep Street.

[13] The Gainsboroughs. The Earl of Gainsborough in Mr. Osborn's time was Charles William Francis Noel. He was born in 1850, and was the third Earl in the second (1841) creation, the first line having become extinct at the death of his great-great-great uncle Henry Noel, sixth Earl under the first creation, in 1798. Charles Noel married twice. His first wife died of puerperal fever in 1877 within a month of the birth of their first child, Agnes Mary Catherine Noel. His second wife was Mary Elizabeth Dease, daughter of James Arthur Dease of Turbotson, Westmeath, Ireland. Mary bore the Earl two daughters - Norah and Clare; and apart from Arthur Edward Joseph Noel, Viscount Campden, she bore him two sons - Charles, and Robert (who died of dysentery in German East Africa in World War One).

[14] Gainsboroughs and Ashbees. The relationship between the Gainsboroughs and Ashbees was never cordial. A typescript history of the Guild by Alec Miller, now in the possession of the Ashbee's daughter,

Felicity Ashbee, mentions that the Gainsboroughs used to visit the Ashbees. Written above this with unmistakeable vigour, is Janet Ashbees's reply: "Never!" An entry in the Ashbee Journals (24 April 1915/213) tells of Mrs. Ashbee, wearing a new dress and taking cover from the rain under an umbrella, being told by the Gainsborough's butler that the family were 'not at home', while listening to their voices in the room beyond.

[15] Frederick Landseer Griggs, R.A. (1876-1938) Dover's Hill. One of England's foremost etchers, renowned for his clear and passionate vision of Gothic England, Griggs first came to Campden in 1904, found congenial company in the orbit of the Guild, and made Campden his life's home. Committed to the traditions and culture of rural England, he was horrified by the march of 'progress' in the period between the wars, and fought to save as much as possible of old Campden. When Dover's Hill - site of the old Cotswold Games (and now of the revived annual Dover's Games) - came up for sale in 1926, it appeared that it would be bought for the construction of a new hotel. Griggs determined to save the Hill. He put his hopes on a fund-raising campaign, and meanwhile made a successful bid for the Hill out of his own funds. Donations came in very slowly, and it was only two years later that Prof. G.M. Trevelyan gave the final amount to meet the purchase price, and the property was then given to the National Trust. Soon after this Griggs bought the property that is now known as Dover's Court, but was then an orchard and farmyard formerly belonging to farmer Ulric Stanley. His idea was to encourage and create a monument to traditions of the local building craft. Dispensing with blueprints, depending upon the skills and good sense of the workmen, he sketched a picture of a beautiful house to be built entirely through manual labour out of local Cotswold Stone. Unfortunately, having committed himself to this project, Griggs lost a substantial part of his income as the Depression hit the American market for his etchings. His last years were particularly desperate ones, the financial impossibilities contributing to his death in 1938. Dover's House was subsequently severely damaged by fire, and was never restored. Four large houses have been built on the grounds. Among those Mr. Osborn considered to have been 'let down' was his brother-in-law, Joe Warmington, a builder who worked on the Dover's House project over the whole period from 1927.

[16] The School. The boys' National School, run under the management of the Church of England, was housed in what is now the Church Rooms opposite the Eight Bells in Church Street. When Mr. Osborn entered the boys' school the headmaster was Albert Crossley. G.W. Dewey, the master

who figures so strongly in Mr. Osborn's memory, took over the school in 1904. Mrs. Dunn, of the Infant's school (now a branch of the County Library in the High Street), is the same Martha Dunn who befriended the Ashbees when they came to Campden. She was a Campden native, having been born into the Haines family, plumbers and metal workers, whose names can be seen pressed into leadwork from St. James' Church on display in the Church Muniment Room. The Boys' School log book of February 9, 1906, notes the arrival of new dual desks for the children, and a new desk for the master.

[17] Almshouse tap/water. This tap is still there, having originally been supplied from the piped water system installed for the Almshouses by Sir Baptist Hicks, c.1612, when the Almshouses were built. The first public water supply was piped into Campden in 1906. A note in the Boys's School logbook for September 10 of that year says that water was laid on into the school at that time, "and a lavatory basin placed in the cloak room." Water closets must have replaced old earth closets about that time. Mr. Don Ellis, who entered the boys' school in 1909, doesn't remember the latter.

[18] present mayor of Campden. In 1979, when Mr Osborn was writing, this was Richard Smith.

[19] Aunt Kathleen. Kathleen Grace Warmington, Harry Warmington's sister and the future Mrs. Osborn. She is "the girl I was selling bread to," mentioned on p.21.

[20] Harry. Harry Warmington, apprenticed in the silversmith shop at the Guild of Handicraft, and went on to become a fine working silversmith and a much loved and respected teacher.

[21] "ever told this to" . Mr. Osborn knew that I might publish his reminiscences in some form, and our agreement was that he would indicate to me whenever a memory or reflection was too private or personal to be published. There are several of these, involving Campden people or himself, which will never be made public. But this story, though it might have embarrassed him a bit when he was alive, was told to me (as well as to Allan Warmington) without any reservations, and that is why I feel it right to include it here. It is a lovely, and genuine, reflection of childhood experience.

[22] Badsey. A market-gardening/agricultural village in Worcestershire, near Evesham, about six miles from Chipping Campden. Harry

Warmington's father had been a market-gardener there.

[23] The Martins door. The front door, and the window in the wall at right angles to it under the porch, have traded places since Mr. Osborn lived in Campden. Instead of entering the Martins with the Market Hall at his back, as would be the case today, Mr. Osborn would have entered with the Market Hall to his right.

[24] Mrs. Morris/Cotswold House. Mr. Osborn is correct, Mrs. E.E. Morris lived in Cotswold House - now the Cotswold House Hotel - until her death in 1912, at which point it was sold for £1,600. Widow of the town doctor, at her death she was also the owner of the adjoining building, Ardeley House; Dial House; and a cottage in Flag Close.

[25] Gabb's. In 1986 the bakery was still in the Gabb family, and their shop was still opposite the corner of Sheep Street, near to where the old Elm Tree stood (see note later). Mrs. Gabb took the bakery and grocery business over when the Heritages retired in 1932, after forty-six years.

[26] Holloway's Theatre. A Holloway's performance was described in Theatre Notebook III, 43, 1948 (p.43): "The theatre was most uncomfortable, with no room to play on the stage, and no proper lights - only candles held by boys who, when engrossed in the performance, dripped wax over players and instruments. The part of Charity was taken by a very fat woman who sat coyly, on a swing which bent dangerously at every movement. It is also recalled that in two of the plays one of the chief male parts was taken by a female; in one case causing some sensation in the audience, as the poor lady, who was clothed in tight fitting red military tunic, was far advanced in pregnancy!" Another note said that the "Holloways were, in their sphere, as numerous and eminent as the Kembles, and claim to trace their ancestors back as portable theatre owners for almost one-hundred and sixty years..."

(Theatre Notebook IV,3,1949, p.3).

[27] Holloways at school. I can't find that the Holloways registered children in the schools in 1905. On July 1, 1907, however, before Mr. Osborn was withdrawn, Evelyn Holloway was admitted to the Infants' School, Florence was admitted to the Girls' School, and William Arthur and Fred Thomas were admitted to the Boys' School. Their father, William, listed his profession as 'actor', and residence as the Noel Yard. A second actor, Ernest Maltravers, registered his daughter Mabel in the Infants' School one week later, on July 8, 1907. All the children were withdrawn

a month later, on August 2nd.

[28] The Campden Wonder. This was a popular theme for travelling theatre players, as were parody versions. John Masefield, a friend and frequent visitor of the Ashbees, later poet laureate, wrote a play of the Campden Wonder in 1906. Hugh Ross Williamsons' fictional treatment of the story in his novel *The Silver Bowl* was used as the basis for a BBC broadcast in 1948, the cast for which included local men Garnet Keyte, Bill Payne, and Lionel Ellis.

The story of the Campden Wonder is strange, but true. In 1660 William Harrison, elderly steward to Lady Juliana Noel of the Court House, Campden, disappeared while collecting rents for his lady. A servant, John Perry, was sent to search for him, but did not return until the next day. Harrison's hat band and comb were found stained with blood, and suspicion fell on John Perry as Harrison's murderer. A search did not turn up the body, but after a week in gaol and contradictory testimony, John Perry confessed to the murder of Harrison by his Mother and Brother, saying that he himself was an accessory. Mother and Brother both protested their innocence, but in 1661 after two trials (the first of which would not convict them of murder because the body had not been found), all three were hanged. Two years later, Harrison returned. He said that he had been kidnapped, put on board a ship which was captured by Turkish pirates, after which he was sold as a slave to an old physician in Smyrna. Upon the death of his master, he made his way home by bribery, fortune and charity. The hanging of the innocent Perry's led to a change in the law. Where Harrison really was, and why John Perry confessed to murder, are mysteries.

[29] Church service in the theatre. "By the kind permission of Mr. Holloway," wrote the *Evesham Journal* of 14 September, 1907, "the Rev. Philip Lewis has conducted two services in the Empire Theatre, on Sunday afternoon, August 25 and September 8. On both occasions the Campden Town Band kindly attended and played anthems, and well-known tunes to favourite hymns. There was a very large attendance, both inside and outside the theatre. At the first service Mr. Lewis gave an address on the Prodigal Son, and at the second he spoke on Decision of Character." At a benefit performance of the play *East Lynne* on August 7, Mr. Holloway had raised £5 for the Campden Nursing Association *(Ev J* 3.8.1907).

[30] Marshal. Mr. Fred Coldicott, who is sixteen years Mr. Osborn's junior, says that this piece of ground was known by everyone as "Marshal's

Grave", and that it is "up on the corner of the Recreation Ground, where it joins the Broad Campden Road." The pile of stones was not there within his memory. Mr. Coldicott has a warrant dated 1806 from George III to the Sheriff of Gloucester for the arrest of Robert Hickman, Richard Keen the Younger, Charles Marshal, and Charles Izod (an ancestor of Mr. Coldicott), for Trespass against Thomas Harris. Is this the Marshal who eventually was hanged and was buried at the crossing?

Mr. Coldicott also tells a true story about Marshal's ghost. One of his old relations, Will Izod (people called him 'Big Shilling') farmed at Broad Campden. There were no motorcars or anything then. The Noel Arms was the meeting place for farmers in those days and Izod used to come on his old pony from Broad Campden, past the grave, and straight down to the back of the Noel Arms on the bridle track. If he had a drop too much, his pony knew the way home. So he set off home one night, sat on his pony. Mr. Coldicott's father, Jack, was a young chap then, and some of them got some old white sheets, and when Big Shilling came along they jumped out of the hedge where Marshal's Grave was supposed to be. Old Izod went like "Hell in the Night" to Broad Campden. And after that night, he swore blind he'd seen old Marshal's ghost.

[31] Yubberton Yawnies. "Yubberton" is the local name of Ebrington, the nearby village with which Campden has been trading friendly abuse for at least a century. It was in Ebrington that they put a fence around the cuckoo to keep in the Spring, put the pig on the wall to see the band go by, and built a bonfire on the church tower to outdo the fire on Dover's Hill - the roofing lead melted, of course, and streamed down the tower walls.

[32] St. Thomas' Day. December 21, the Winter Solstice, a traditional day in England for charity and almsgiving. In Campden it is still marked by a distribution of bread to all the householders in Leaseborne. Before the turn of the century the children of Campden took the day as a holiday from school, with or without the blessing of the teacher (school in those days could break up anything up to Christmas Eve, and might resume within several days). The school log books mention children taking unofficial holidays to collect "Christmas boxes", or pence. The Vicar and others in Campden tried to stop the school-leaving by sending pence, oranges and buns to any children who were in school on St. Thomas' Day. This strategy apparently worked, if Mr. Osborn is correct - or perhaps Northwick Park provided a superior attraction to making the rounds of Campden? In any event, around the turn of the century December 21

disappears from the log books as a special day of attendance trouble.

[33] Northwick Park. The seat of the Rushout family, Barons Northwick, in the parish of Blockley. Lady Northwick was the widow of George, third Baron Northwick, who died in 1887 leaving no male heirs, the title therefore becoming extinct. When Lady Northwick died in 1912, she left the property to her son-in-law, Capt. Edward George Spencer-Churchill. The Park had 300 acres. There were two sizeable lakes, well stocked with fish. Before the First World War there was also a herd of 500 fallow deer. A main attraction of Northwick was its picture gallery, which was opened to the local public on special occasions. In it were paintings by Hogarth, Rubens, Titian, Raphael, Landseer, Giotto, Velasquez, etc.

[34] old mansion. The remains of Old Campden House, the country seat built for himself near the Church by Sir Baptist Hicks, but burned by departing royalists in 1645 .

[35] mummers. Records show that Campden has had its Christmas mummers for over a century, and family tradition in the Tomes, Buckland and Benfield families (who have been largely responsible for the custom's survival in this century) carries it back for a hundred and fifty years, at least. The fact that Mr. Osborn was not aware of them does not mean they didn't exist. Traditionally, the Campden mummers have gone unannounced to private houses during the Christmas season, and caught the occupants by surprise with their play, and the songs and stories which often follow. Many people living in Campden today are not aware that the mummers still go out, and a good many long-time residents had never had the opportunity of seeing the traditional side perform until the Chamber of Trade initiated a regular pre-Christmas Victorian Street Market a few years ago at which they have performed.

[36] Morris dancing. Chipping Campden has one of the best-known sides of traditional morris dancers in the country. A boy's team, trained by Dennis Hathaway, danced before Cecil Sharp in 1910, but there are records of morris dancers as early as the late eighteenth century. The current side dances for many charitable events, and is annually a central feature of the town's Scuttlebrook Wake

[37] Maypole : dormant. It seems to have been last performed prior to 1903 at the Whitsun Floral Fete and parade in 1897

[38] Maypole today. The maypole is danced every year at Scuttlebrook Wake in the Market Square by the children from St. James' Church of

England Primary School - and has been, as Mr. Osborn points out, for almost the whole of this century. Children from St. Catherines's Roman Catholic School traditionally perform country and ethnic dances.

[39] Empire Day. Empire Day was first celebrated in 1902 on the late Queen Victoria's birthday - May 24th - and sometimes blended in with the Whitsun holidays. It was meant to train the school-children in good citizenship and appreciation of the Empire. Among the songs sung locally in Campden, and still remembered in 1986, is one that begins "What is the meaning of Empire Day/Why do the cannons roar?". Since 1958 it has been called Commonwealth Day, and has been transferred to the present Queen's official birthday.

[40] "opposition god" . Fiona McCarthy, *The Simple Life*, p.148.

[41] "doom for aristocracy" . The same as the above.

[42] Viscount Campden. Born in 1884, Arthur Edward Joseph became the 4th Earl of Gainsborough on the death of his father, 17 April, 1926. He, in turn, died the following year, on 27 August 1927. The double death duties were a severe blow. The current Earl of Gainsborough was born in 1923, and had not yet turned four years old when his father died.

[43] Sunday School teacher. This was Herbert Wixey, whose shop at the corner of High Street and Church Street is now a private dwelling. He was a man of many parts. Mrs. Ashbee wrote a letter to her husband on April 28, 1902, describing her first encounter with this Sunday School teacher: "Got three sovereigns from the Bank long after Bank hours on consideration of buying 1lb bacon!! The Bank Manager Mr. Wixey (alias Manager of Gas Co. alias China and glass provider alias grocer), shook hands with me with great fervour over the counter and sent me a present of tea!!" C.R. Ashbee wrote of Wixey to his wife some years later in a somewhat less enthusiastic vein (October 7, 1911): "That dreadful Gas Co, relaying its mains had suddenly taken into the said space where should be its head, to lay them precisely through the roots of the trees. Everybody has been up in arms and down in the ditches ... The lime tree *(near Bedfont House)* will I think be destroyed, the Gingko tree I have saved by threatening the foreman with the police and making everybody at separate intervals call upon the unconscionable Wixey and ask him why? The town now has enough to talk about for three weeks." A number of trees were planted along High Street towards the end of the last century in a bid to make the town more attractive for visitors and potential new residents.

The Gingko, a relative of the yew, native to the Far East and rarely found in England, had been planted by the solicitor W.H. Griffiths, of Bedfont House.

[44] Garnet Keyte. Working in his father's coal business and then taking it over, as well as developing a line in market gardening, Mr. Keyte achieved a kind of fame with several other local men who regularly appeared in BBC broadcasts from the 1930's on. His first broadcast was also the first programme in the "Microphone at Large" series, a live collection of Campden characters and customs, from F.L. Griggs' new Dover's House on October 17, 1934. Keyte played Gaffer Pearce in the 1937 broadcast of John Masefield's play "The Tragedy of Nan", and in the same year was in the first of a series of programmes written by C.H. Gardiner on life in a Cotswold village. The programme was titled "Pump and Circumstance", and also featured Campden residents Percy Dewey, Bill Payne, Lionel Ellis and George Hart. He died in 1971, at the age of 87.

[45] Algy Hathaway. Among the sixty Campden men killed in the First World War, he was a member of the football team (The Excels) and of the town band, and for a short time worked in the Guild of Handicraft. C. R. Ashbee wrote about him in his *Journals* (15.11.1914/359), at the outset of the Great War: "Algy has probably never read Shakespeare, but he can sing, and he can dance the Morris, he has a fine sense of humour and an abounding humanity ... there are always small boys about him listening to his stories ... No one rode the hobby horse or danced in the High Street so well as Algy..." Dennis, his older brother, leader of the Morris dancers "is too old now for the front, but Algy will take the dance with him into the trenches."

Algy wrote a letter to his mother from the front (in the Dardanelles) part of which was printed in the *Evesham Journal* (11.9.1915) : "It is terrible hot out here. We dare not say where we are, but we are in the thick of it. I hope it will soon be over. I hope everything is going on all right at home. I am all right up to the time I post this, and I hope God will spare me to get through safe. I should not care for foreign life. Give me old England before any of it." Less than a year out of Campden, on the seventh of August, 1915, he was killed.

[46] Teapot. James "Teapot" Williams, one of Campden's best known 'characters', who ate mice live (as I've been told), and gained national notoriety in a broadcast of Wilfred Pickles' popular radio programme "Have a Go", recorded in Campden at the end of 1948. Wilfred Pickles asked

him who he'd like to be, and after thinking a bit, Teapot replied: "What's 'is name, up in London - the man as smokes the cigars". After this reference to Winston Churchill he received a sizeable number of cigars through the post. It's said that he didn't have a proper mug to drink out of, and always drank out of a little kettle. He himself said he got the name off his uncle, a roadman of the same name with whom he used to work picking stones off the road. When his uncle "pegged out", Teapot is quoted as saying *(Ev J 2.10.1948)*, the name passed to him. He himself died in 1953.

[47] Corn laws. Presumably those of 1815, which restricted the importation of foreign corn until home wheat prices reached a set price. In harness with the bad harvests of 1816 and 1837-42, this caused a great deal of economic distress, and presumably the land would have gone out of cultivation then. In 1849 the law was repealed, and the corn market returned to a free-trade footing.

[48] Trees/meeting places. The old Elm Tree which, until 1973, stood opposite Sheep Street Corner, was used as a meeting place throughout the nineteenth century - for church services, political rallies, and the like. About the time Joseph Arch visited Campden, organising for the National Agricultural Labourers' Union in 1872, the tree was styled 'The Union Tree'. Another name was 'The Gospel Tree', and perhaps this latter led to its disuse as a public speaker's corner. In 1899 a Wesleyan lay minister named R.M. Kedward, a "Joyful News" evangelist, was brought up before the Campden magistrates for disturbing the peace with his preaching at the Elm Tree. The magistrates, of course, were all Church of England, and a question was raised on the case in the House of Commons. The Home Secretary was asked to explain the apparent suppression of open-air preaching, particularly of Non-Conformists, by State-Church magistrates. Kedward was sent to prison for a month without hard labour, refusing to pay the fine, but a friend bailed him out. Protest services were held under the Elm tree. Referring to the Kedward case, the *Midland Free Churchman*, quoted in the *Evesham Journal* of 5.8.1899, claimed, "Under cover of certain County Bye-laws attempts are being made, in various parts of the country, to suppress open-air preaching." Perhaps, then, by the time that Mr. Osborn arrived in 1902 the customary right of using the tree as a meeting-site had been suppressed.

[49] Pump/chestnut tree. The chestnut tree, planted in 1812, fell onto a showman's caravan at Scuttlebrook Wake in 1932, having been undermined by heavy rains. The pump was removed, but no better site having been

found for it, was eventually returned. According to architect Guy Pemberton, writing at the time *(Ev J 8.10.1932)*, "This particular pump, which is of pure Adams design ... is one of the earliest examples of the time when art was first brought to bear on objects of public utility." The pump was given to Campden in 1832 by the Rev. Leland Noel.

[50] Sculpture. Mr. Osborn is right, the old mansion will have been a wonderful quarry for dressed stone, but the features he mentions are more likely Georgian than Elizabethan. Much of the High Street is of 18th century construction or re-facing.

[51] Town crier. An indispensable source of local advertisement and announcement. When the Guild arrived in 1902, the town crier was Thomas Smith, who was also the rural postman. Up to 1986, Campden's town crier was Laurence Ladbrook (son of the Edwin Ladbrook, butcher, mentioned in an earlier note), who first retired in 1963 after thirty years at the job, then returned in 1974, his last public appearance being in 1981. In 1986 a new Town Crier, Seumas Stewart, was appointed and still (in 1996) cries when occasion demands.

The comic side of the Campden town crier was discovered by a writer signing himself 'Kark' in the Christmas, 1881, issue of the Grammar School's magazine, *The Campdonian:*

> Dingle-ding - dingle-ding - dingle-dong. Hush! every ear is strained, every breath stopped in silent expectancy. "To be sould amundreny ofentre peegsafitt," (lost to posterity owing to the noise of a passing cart) "to commence ateacron," and so this relic of the barbarous ages goes his way, disseminating valuable information at every corner. Mrs. Graggles wants to buy a mangle, "cheap", so she listens to what comes next, "amundreny ofentre," "Oh furniture, I think he says," she softly whispers "wherever is it, I wonder," listens, "peegsafitt." "Wherever is peegsafitt?" "Perhaps it isn't furniture at all, but pigs feet to be sold." Listens attentively, "ba", "ba", calls out an old sheep as he goes by. "Bother that sheep," says Mrs. G. "I've just missed the very part I wanted to hear." "To commence at ateacron" winds up the now exhausted bellman. "Oh ateacron, ateacron is it to begin you might just as well have said at treacle pie or batter pudding for all I can hear of you," fairly bursts out the now exasperated Mrs. Gaggles (her mind running on last Sunday's dinner) as coolly wiping his mouth, and putting his bell under his arm, Mr. Crier moves on his way.

[52] period under discussion. Alan Crawford sent Mr. Osborn several chapters of his book, *C.R. Ashbee* (Yale University Press, 1985), in early-draft for his comments and contributions. Here, Mr. Osborn is remarking on the period before the Guild moved to Campden, before he had any personal contact with C.R. Ashbee.

[53] Craftsmanship in Competitive Industry. By C.R. Ashbee, published by his Essex House Press, Campden, in 1908. This book was an epitaph, apology, and argument for the future of his ideas, springing out of the collapse of the Guild. As with Ashbee's work generally, it is a combined product of shrewd and brilliant insight, romanticism, and propaganda for a cause he deeply believed in.

[54] Alec Miller. One of the Ashbee's closest disciples, began work at the age of 12 in a Glasgow slum, and went on from the Guild of Handicraft to become an internationally known sculptor/wood-carver. He died in 1961, on C.R. Ashbee's birthday, and the day that the ashes of Janet Ashbee (who had just died) "were sent down for the committal service to the church in Seal where she and Charley had been married..." (Fiona McCarthy, *The Simple Life*, p. 184). See also Jane Wilgress's study *Alec Miller: Guildsman and Sculptor in Chipping Campden*, (CADHAS, 1987)

[55] triplets. If Mr. Osborn is right about Mrs. Jack Bailey having a set of triplets after the move to Stratford, then the papers might well make a to-do of it. According to the *Evesham Journal* of 11 June 1910, the Baileys had a set of three boys, all healthy, while they were still living in Catbrook in Campden.

[56] Marie Corelli. (1855~1924). The most popular novelist of her day : her novel *The Sorrows of Satan* (1895) broke all previous sales records. She lived in her house in Stratford-on-Avon from 1901 until her death.

[57] School of Arts and Crafts. The Guild was actually taking over the County Council grant for public evening technical education administered by the Campden Grammar School since 1891. What the Guild brought to it were its own brand of idealism, and lectures in Art, Music, Literature and History. In short, the Guild grafted a liberal arts course onto an existing programme of technical education.

[58] picture. *The Simple Life* plate 9.

[59] bathing lake. The possibility of a public bathing place was raised as

early as 1886, but the serious initiative to establish a Campden Bathing Lake began with the parish meeting of 1898, when the Grammar School headmaster, F.B.Osborne (no relation to Harry Osborn), put forward the motion that the parish council consider building one. He said that he had already tried to find a site for a private bathing pool for the school, but had run into problems. The meeting passed his resolution, and the parish council acted on it. A site in the Coneygree was vetoed by the Earl of Gainsborough as too exposed and difficult of access. A natural depression on a stream past Westington Mill was suggested, but this possibility bogged down in the problem of costs in 1901. When the Guild arrived in the following year, and it was discovered that C.R. Ashbee and Robert Holland-Martin were willing to lend the money to build the lake, this is apparently the site chosen. The bathing lake opened in August 1903. Eleven years later, at the outbreakof the Great War, £67 was still owing Ashbee and Holland-Martin.

[60] Broad Campden Pool. This bathing pool came on the market in 1971, and the parish council tried to raise the funds to buy and keep it open. A couple from Herefordshire bought it, but planning restrictions and local official resistance prevented the pool's reopening

[61] carol-singing. The money collected went to buy season tickets to the bathing lake for the children involved.

[62] Ted Horwood. Jeweller, began work with the Guild in 1897, and was elected a Guildsman in 1902.

[63] Thomas Binning. Compositor with the Essex House Press, became a Guildsman in 1899.

[64] Walter Curtis. Cabinet maker. Next to Ashbee himself, Walter Curtis was the longest-serving member of the Guild of Handicraft in Campden. He began with the Guild in 1888, becoming a full Guildsman in 1889.

[65] Present mayor of Campden. In 1982, when Mr. Osborn wrote this letter, this was Richard Smith.

[66] Anne Power. Bookbinder. Worked with the Guild from 1902-1906, without becoming a full Guildsman.

[67] W.J. Osborn. Served thirteen years with the Guild, having become a Guildsman in 1892, ten years before the move to Campden.

[68] mother's experience. This subject arose naturally out of Mr. Osborn's

memories of 'ghosts' (see page 16), as we shared experiences we'd had or knew of. I told him of an experience I'd had when away at school. Robert Kennedy was running for the presidential nomination. My roommate and I had put a Kennedy campaign poster on the wall and over it had hung a hangman's noose. One night it all fell off the wall. The next morning we heard the news that Kennedy had been killed just about the time our poster and noose had fallen down. Mr. Osborn's daughter tells me that Mr. Osborn kept a clock on his mantlepiece, which kept time perfectly for many years. She took it home as a memento, and despite being properly wound, it has since regularly stopped at midnight. She wonders if that is the time at which her father died.

[69] Lloyd Francis. Mr Osborn's daughter wrote in September 1985 that Mr. Francis was then the Canadian ambassador to Portugal, and that he and her father had indeed (to her surprise) been friends.

[70] Christopher Whitfield. Mr. Whitfield's reference, in his *A History of Chipping Campden*, (Shakespeare Head Press, Windsor, 1958 p. 249) reads (in full): "Two years later in May 1908 His Majesty King Edward VII, while staying at Batsford with Lord Redesdale, drove over 'in his own motor car' and visited the town, though but briefly, on his way to Stanway. The visit was enlivened by an occurrence at Broad Campden, which may well have amused the King. Campden's newspaper-seller, Bob Dickinson, a thin, comical character at the time, though he fell into a melancholy in his old age, stepped out into the road as the royal car slowly rounded the corner by the Norman Chapel at Broad Campden, stopped the car and insisted on selling the King a paper - after which he painted a version of the Royal Arms on his canvas paper-bag and claimed to be a purveyor to Royalty, a distinction upon which he insisted to the amusement of visitors for many a year after."

[71] Date of King's visit. Actually, King Edward VII visited Batsford Park on July 8, 1905, an event the *Evesham Journal* hailed "as historical". The *Journal* even added a special photographic supplement as a souvenir of the event to its July 17, 1905, issue. "The tradition of the great British Monarchy," wrote the *Journal* editor, "and the fame and glory of the world-wide British Empire, can never be detached from the person of the King in whatever guise he meets his people. But in this particular instance, in this unceremonious visit to a friend, a deeper personal note was struck and one of the most happy augury to this Kingdom. The King is doubly enthroned, not only as the Monarch of his people, but also in their hearts

as their personal friend. Such a position is the strongest possible in the relations of King and Subject..."

Writing to her husband on June 28, just over a week before the visit, Janet Ashbee said: "The teachers' tea has been postponed till the 15th July, on account of his most religious and Gracious Majesty's visit to Moreton on the 8th which appears to inebriate all the surrounding villages and towns. I wonder if we shall feel any reflex wash from the sailing by of such a craft?"

The reflex wash of the Bob Dickinson affair - taken in the light of the *Journal* editorial - is preserved in Mr Osborn's story not as a quaint example of rustic impropriety, but as an example of the life of the local community and the friendly relations between subject and monarch. The *News of the World* took a third moral from its version of the story - a moral which is, not surprisingly, self-advertising:

> *Our Royal Reader: King Edward and the "News of the World"*. King Edward last week paid a week-end visit to Lord Redesdale at Batsford Park, Moreton-in-Marsh, Glos. On Sunday, as His Majesty in his motor-car was going through the village of Broad Campden, where several hundreds of spectators had gathered to view the Royal Progress, Mr. Robert Dickinson, of Cider Mill Lane, Chipping Campden, the "News of the World" agent, carrying his bag of papers, was passed by the Royal car. Mr. Dickinson immediately brandished a parcel of "News of the World" papers, and waved them to the occupants of the motor. The party, who had seen the printed bag on Mr. Dickinson's back, at once caused the car to be stopped, and, drawing up within 100 yards of Mr. Dickinson, one of the suite descended. Mr. Dickinson thereupon presented a copy of the "News of the World" to the gentleman, who, with a salute, handed it to the King, His Majesty accepting it with evident pleasure. The incident caused not a little excitement amongst the village crowd, who cheered Mr Dickinson as well as the Royal party. *(News of the World*, July 16, 1905, p.4)

[72] Lord Redesdale. A personal friend of the King, to visit whom the King had come to Batsford Park, near Blockley. They were friends from youth, when Lord Redesdale was still Algernon Bertram Freeman Mitford, and the noble title still in the possession of his cousin. His cousin died in 1886, with no male issue, and the title became extinct. The property and fortune, however, passed to Algernon, who left Chelsea (where he was a neighbour, if not an aquaintance, of C.R. Ashbee), and took up residence

at Batsford Park. He had the old mansion torn down and a new one built, and exercised his considerable talent in landscape gardening. He was a Japan expert, author, and something of an antiquarian, who was on good terms with the Ashbees, and gave the opening speech at the School of Arts and Crafts in its 1905 session. His daughter, Frances, and Janet Ashbee seem to have gotten on well. He was also the grandfather of the well-known Nancy Mitford and sisters. He was raised to the peerage by his friend the King in 1902, as the lst Baron Redesdale in the second creation.

INDEX

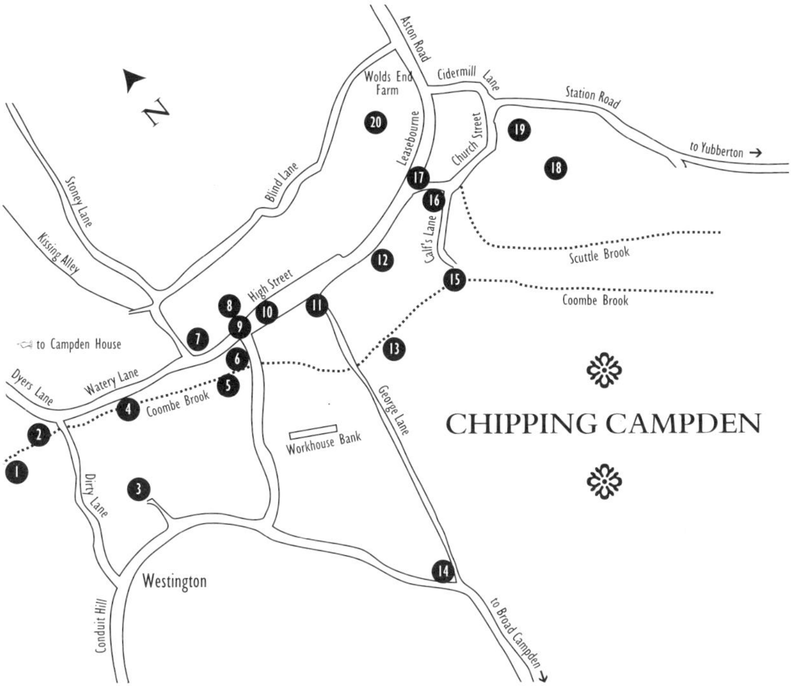

MAP OF CHIPPING CAMPDEN IN 1905

Key:

1. The Bathing Lake
2. Westington Mill
3. Heavenley Corner
4. The Osborns' House, Watery Lane
5. The Silk Mill
6. The Osborns' House, 6 Sheep Street
7. The Catholic Church
8. Elm Tree House: the School of Arts & Crafts
9. The Elm Tree
10. The Craftsman's Club
11. The Noel Arms
12. The Grammar School
13. Badgers Field
14. Marshal's Grave
15. Haydon's Mill
16. The Boys' Elementary School
17. The Chestnut Tree
18. Haydon's Orchard; Old Campden House
19. St. James's Parish Church
20. Dovers Court